The Research Virtuoso

Brilliant Methods for Normal Brains

TORONTO PUBLIC LIBRARY

art by Joe Weissmann

ANNICK PRESS LTD.

Toronto • New York • Vancouver

©2006 Toronto Public Library (text)
©2006 Joe Weissmann (art)
Design: Sheryl Shapiro
Researched and written by Ab. Velasco, Toronto Public Library
Edited by Barbara Czarnecki

Annick Press Ltd.

We acknowledge the support of the Canada Council for the Arts, the Ontario Arts Council, and the Government of Canada through the Book Publishing Industry Development Program (BPIDP) for our publishing activities.

Cataloging in Publication

The research virtuoso : brilliant methods for normal brains / Toronto Public Library ; art by Joe Weissmann.

Includes bibliographical references and index.
ISBN-13: 978-1-55037-957-0 (bound)
ISBN-10: 1-55037-957-7 (bound)
ISBN-13: 978-1-55037-956-3 (pbk.)
ISBN-10: 1-55037-956-9 (pbk.)

1. Research—Methodology—Handbooks, manuals, etc. 2. Information retrieval—Handbooks, manuals, etc. 3. Library research—Handbooks, manuals, etc. I. Weissmann, Joe, 1947- II. Toronto Public Library

ZA3075.R46 2006   001.4'2   C2005-907823-5

The text was typeset in Galliard.

Distributed in Canada by:
Firefly Books Ltd.
66 Leek Crescent
Richmond Hill, ON
L4B 1H1

Published in the U.S.A. by Annick Press (U.S.) Ltd.
Distributed in the U.S.A. by:
Firefly Books (U.S.) Inc.
P.O. Box 1338
Ellicott Station
Buffalo, NY 14205

Printed in Canada.

Visit us at: www.annickpress.com

In *The Research Virtuoso*, you will find a list of recommended websites for research. With the exception of Virtual Reference Library, these websites are not endorsed by Annick Press or Toronto Public Library.

Also, please note that although these websites were current and functional when this book went to press, web addresses do change all the time. If you come across a dead link, try typing just the first part of the address – up to the first slash (/) – where applicable. This takes you to the site host's home page.

Contents

From a topic to a final product: learn the tried-and-true steps to masterful research and sound documentation. *Plus, Part 1 of the saga of Dominic, the budding Research Virtuoso.*

Use search engines and subject directories, find information located in the deep Web, access multimedia files, read an e-book or e-journal, and learn how to evaluate all these sources. *Plus, Dominic logs on to the Web to find the goods.*

Discover the many avenues to information on your library website – catalog, subject guides, online references, tutorials, and more. Log on to library databases and digital collections to find information quicker than ever before. *Plus, Dominic explores his library's website.*

Not all the good stuff's on the Net. Explore the rich resources in your library, including reference collections and services for researchers. Use special collections and archives to find rare or unique items. *Plus, Dominic's quest to become a Research Virtuoso reaches its climax.*

Wait! Before you hand in your assignment, use our handy checklist – with tips from a university professor – so that all your bases are covered. *Plus, Dominic reads the reviews.*

Acknowledgments

The year 2005 has been an unbelievable time of fun and learning, all thanks to the support of Toronto Public Library and Annick Press. Thank you Ken Setterington for the hilarious anecdotes and Barbara Czarnecki for superb and precise feedback. Thank you Joe Weissmann and Sheryl Shapiro for making such a splendid looking book.

This book has also benefited from the input of Lesley Bell, Stephanie Boyd, Kelly Donaldson, Cecile Farnum, Luba Frastacky, Erin Holman, Deborah Kay, Greg Kelner, Mary LeQuoc, Mark Moss, Elsa Ngan, Paulette Rothbauer, Arthur Schwartzel, Mary Shantz, Lisa Sherlock, Lisa Singer, Joyce Smith, Ken Sparling, and Ron Stagg.

Thank you Patricia Eastman and Peggy Sinclair for going the extra mile.

Much thanks to the TPL Foundation staff (Karen, Kim, Liza, Heather, Anna, Debi, Catherine) for the wonderful work environment and food.

Lastly, thanks to Andrew, Harley, and kittyboi for the moral support.

—Ab. Velasco

Foreword

Imagine signing out your own librarian. Imagine a knowledgeable guide who shows you how to find the best reliable information on the Internet, in the library, and beyond. Imagine a specialist who keeps in touch with the latest trends and resources, just so you can benefit from them. In *The Research Virtuoso*, Toronto Public Library brings you some of a librarian's expertise in a compact guide so that you too can be a research superstar.

In September 2005, *Research Ate My Brain* — the Toronto Public Library's research handbook for teens — was released in bookstores across North America. When Annick Press approached the Library about collaborating on a follow-up book for older readers, it was a natural next step.

The Library sees every day that the thirst and quest for information is not limited to any age group. The text, sidebars, and tips in this book can be used by researchers of all ages and applied to any research task – whether for school, business, or personal interests.

In addition to consultation with TPL users and staff, the Library gathered valuable input from instructors and librarians from academic institutions. The Library would like to thank Ab. Velasco for his hard work in researching and writing the manuscript.

With *The Research Virtuoso*, the librarian steps out from behind the reference desk and joins you in discovering exciting worlds of knowledge.

—Josephine Bryant
City Librarian, Toronto Public Library

Chapter 1

Getting Ready for Research

A journey of a thousand miles begins with one step. For a researcher today, that first step usually takes place on the Internet, from the comfort of the home computer. Search engines, such as Google, can help you find information on the Internet. But Google isn't the only search engine, and there are also plenty of other research tools that you might not know about.

Research can be a challenging process, but it can also be quite rewarding. You are about to learn a lot, and not just about the topic you're looking into.

Dominic:
The Budding Virtuoso

Dominic is a first-year college student facing his first big essay assignment in the fall of 2006. The topic is: "Can genetically modified crops help feed the poor in Africa?"

He's used to Google (www.google.com), so that's where he starts. But after he types in *GM Africa*, he gets over 4.5 million results — too much of a good thing! And actually, some of the web pages are about General Motors. Although some results are related to his topic (e.g., GMWatch.org), he can see that he needs to upgrade his research skills if he's going to meet his deadline.

HOW TO GET STARTED: THE OVERVIEW

Wouldn't it be great if everything you needed were available in one source and in one place? Too bad it never works like that.

Research is like detective work. You have to find pieces of information from different places. You will also need to use analytical skills to evaluate your information. Sometimes you'll realize that you've found a false lead. Eventually you will decide how the pieces fit together. When you solve the case, it will feel great.

So where do you start? Professors and librarians recommend looking for an overview of your topic first. Use general reference works such as encyclopedias and dictionaries to understand the terms and main concepts of your topic. Look for summary information that will help you understand the big picture before you look for smaller pieces. See the General References sidebar below for more on this subject.

GENERAL REFERENCE SOURCES PROVIDE AN OVERVIEW

Here are reference sources that can give you an overview (summary information) for your topic. They are available in print; some are also available online (see chapter 2) and in electronic databases (see chapter 3).

- **Almanacs, Factbooks, Yearbooks** — Find statistics, facts, and lists in works such as *The World Factbook*, published by the U.S. Central Intelligence Agency (CIA).
- **Atlases** — Find maps and geographical facts in *The National Atlas of the United States of America*, *The National Atlas of Canada*, etc.
- **Biographical Directories** — Find information about a person's life (*Who's Who in America*, etc.).
- **Dictionaries** — Find definitions, correct spelling, and pronunciation of terms. Some dictionaries cover more specific fields of knowledge (*Blackwell Dictionary of Sociology*, for instance).
- **Encyclopedias** — Find summary information on general knowledge (*Encyclopaedia Britannica*, etc.). Some encyclopedias cover particular subjects (*Encyclopedia of Philosophy*).

Consult a subject guide (see page 44) or ask a librarian to find special reference works in the subject area you're researching.

Many reference sources are available on the Internet (see chapter 2) or in your library's electronic resources (see chapter 3). An advantage of using these resources is that they permit more efficient searches. Libraries also have extensive collections of reference works in print (see chapter 4).

Not sure which reference source to consult? You can refer to the **subject guides** available online or in print at your library (see page 44). These guides, prepared by librarians, list recommended sources for various subjects. You can also ask your instructors or librarians for specific suggestions.

Dominic needs overview information. He starts with a search on Encyclopedia.com, which provides free content from the *Columbia Encyclopedia* (Sixth Edition). He types in *genetic modification*. The second result is an article that explains the science of genetic engineering. He verifies with Dictionary.com that the two terms are synonyms.

On the same Encyclopedia.com results page, he finds an article on *biotechnology* — another term related to genetic modification. As he does with all online sources, Dominic prints the page and files it in a folder. He also adds the web page to his Favorites, in a folder called GM Essay.

In the Encyclopaedia Britannica website (www.britannica.com), which he has full access to through school, a search for *genetically modified crops* finds an article titled "Genetically Modified Foods: The Political Debate." This gives Dominic a sense of the controversy surrounding his topic. He will need to examine the differing viewpoints to get the whole picture.

Africa is a huge continent that Dominic knows little about at this point. To get an idea of the poverty picture there, he goes to the Information Please website (www.infoplease.com), which provides an almanac, atlas, dictionary, encyclopedia, and thesaurus. In the almanac, he clicks on *World Statistics*. Two documents, titled "World's 50 Poorest Countries" (2004) and "Economic Statistics by Countries" (2004), have some telling facts and figures.

Dominic now has a rough idea of where the poorest African countries are, but he wants to see the regions and other geographical characteristics that some sources have referred to. At the nearby library he takes a look at the *Canadian Oxford World Atlas* (Fifth Edition). In addition to political and physical maps, Dominic finds thematic maps such as climate regions, economic development, and agricultural trends. They give him a better understanding of "sub-Saharan" Africa, the area where agriculture is most challenged.

Tip

Think Ahead about Electronic Searches
Keep a list in your notebook or a computer file of key terms and concepts you identify in your overview research. Add to it as you find synonyms or new ideas. You'll need to try lots of different terms when you do electronic searches.

RESEARCH IN DEPTH: THE VIRTUOSO'S SECRETS

Once you have an overview of your topic, search for in-depth information to flesh it out. We have organized everything you need to know about research tools and resources into three chapters.

THE INTERNET

Search online for websites and other electronic sources, such as audio and video files. Most students today start their research by using popular Internet search engines, but you might not know how to get the most out of your searches when working on an academic assignment.

In chapter 2, learn how to find specific, reliable information efficiently by using online tools such as search engines and subject directories. We also discuss online resources such as e-books and e-journals.

THE VIRTUAL LIBRARY

Use your academic or public library's website and other online resources — the virtual library — to find information quickly, easily, and for free.

In chapter 3, learn how your library provides access to resources on the Internet. For instance, you will learn how to use the library's databases to find articles and books in an electronic format. The online resources in the virtual library have been filtered and organized by information specialists, which makes your research tasks simpler.

THE INFORMATION WAREHOUSE

Visit your public or academic library to find print resources including books, magazines, and journals, and items in other formats such as DVDs and CD-ROMs.

In chapter 4, learn how to use the online catalog to search for these items. You will also learn about special collections and archives where you can find rare and historical information, and about library services that can make you a better researcher.

THE ABCs OF EVALUATING INFORMATION

Your work will be judged largely by the quality of your information. As you find potential sources, it is important to consider if each one is reliable or appropriate for your topic. Look for the ABCs of Evaluating Sources checklists in chapters 2 to 4. They will guide you in evaluating the sources you find both on and off the Internet.

DOCUMENTATION DOS AND DON'TS

Good researchers and writers acknowledge the work of others by using proper documentation. You can give credit to the sources where you got your information by placing data that you copy word for word between quotation marks, by using notes or parenthetical citations, and by creating a Works Cited list.

The two documentation styles you likely know from high school come from the Modern Language Association (MLA) and the American Psychological Association (APA). Other styles you might use in college or university include Chicago Style, Council of Biology Editors (CBE) Style, and Turabian Style (see the Documentation Styles sidebar on page 12).

Your instructors will specify what style you should use. But the basic rule is always the same: cite your sources.

TRACK BIBLIOGRAPHIC DATA AS YOU GO

Develop the habit of keeping track of bibliographic data (author, title, publication information, page numbers) as you do your research. You'll save yourself the time and trouble of looking up your sources again later just to find missing information that you need for your Works Cited list.

Familiarize yourself with the documentation style you will use so that you know what pieces of information to record for each source. For instance, the MLA style requires the date on which you retrieve an article from a database (the **access date**); but the Chicago style does not generally include access dates for periodical articles in databases.

DOCUMENTATION STYLES

Refer to your academic library's print and electronic guides to the various documentation styles. Check out the selected resources below too. Campus bookstores carry most documentation style guides in print.

• **Modern Language Association** (www.mla.org/style) — The official website includes a page where students can purchase the latest MLA handbook.

• **American Psychological Association** (www.apa.org) — The official website includes a page where students can purchase the latest APA style guide.

• **E-Reference** (ereference.uwaterloo.ca) — Click on *Citation/Style Guides* to find a list of links compiled by the University of Waterloo. These links point you to the standard style guides — MLA, APA, Chicago, CBE, and Turabian — and more.

AUTOMATED DOCUMENTATION

Your school may provide access to electronic tools that make documentation easier. For example, RefWorks is a web-based bibliographic citation manager that helps you to collect, store, and organize citations for your sources. RefWorks then formats your paper and Works Cited list to any style you specify.

But even if you use a resource like RefWorks, it's good to record the bibliographic data in another form too, as backup. See the tips below.

TRY THESE TRACKING TIPS

- Create a heading on a page of a computer document or notebook for each of the sources you use, before you take notes from it. Use the heading to list whatever bibliographic data you need for your Works Cited list.
- Bookmark a website where you've found useful information. To do this, click on the icon marked Favorites or Bookmarks. You'll be able to revisit these websites easily to verify your facts and gather bibliographic data.
- Photocopy pages containing bibliographic information from print sources. For example, keep a copy of the title and copyright pages of a book or the table of contents from a journal. They contain most of the bibliographic data you need.
- Print out electronic documents. The print date will be included at the bottom of each page; this is the access date. Unless the bibliographic data you need is included with the document, write it down at the top of the first page.

Dominic is more confident about where he is going with his research. From his overview research, he has constructed a list — in a computer document — of the terms he has come across, so that he can use them in his searches.

His instructor has specified the MLA style for documenting his sources. Dominic has the most recent edition of the *MLA Handbook for Writers of Research Papers* (Joseph Gibaldi, 2003) handy. He creates a computer file to use for taking notes. He makes a heading with each source's bibliographic information, as specified in MLA, and below it he types out in point form the notes he needs from that source. He starts his documentation with the sources he has just used for his overview research.

PLAGIARUS: LATIN FOR "KIDNAPPER"

Do you like to write, draw, or take pictures? Imagine that you have just finished a work you've been slaving over for weeks. Feels great, doesn't it? Now imagine that someone snatches your work and passes it off as their own. How do you feel now?

That's what plagiarism is. Harvard University defines *plagiarism* as "passing off a source's information, ideas, or words as your own by omitting to cite them." Look for your own school's definition in the student code of conduct, which will be on the website or in your student handbook.

What constitutes plagiarism may not be obvious. For instance, if you change a few words around from a source, that's paraphrasing; if you pass the original source text off as your own work, it's plagiarism. If you cut-and-paste information from different websites and piece it together without proper documentation, it's plagiarism.

Sometimes the pressure to get a good grade may make "borrowing" someone else's work look tempting. But the consequences of plagiarism may be costly. They include failing an assignment, failing a course, or expulsion. To avoid even unintentional plagiarism, document or cite your sources clearly. Don't throw away any files or papers until after you've received your assignment back, in case you are accused of plagiarism. Good documentation of your work — your *own* work — is your best defense.

THE RIGHT WAY

Plagiarism can take many forms, and some may not be obvious. Cite — give credit to — your sources to avoid falling into the plagiarism trap.

- Use quotation marks around words that you copy exactly.
- Cite direct quotations, like this observation by Oscar Wilde: "All that I desire to point out is the general principle that Life imitates Art far more than Art imitates Life."
- Cite statistics, summaries from abstracts, or distinct information from an organization's website, such as this excerpt from the Toronto Public Library's

About Us page: "The Toronto Public Library is the largest public library system in Canada with 99 branches and more than 11 million items . . ."

- Cite distinct ideas. You don't need to cite common knowledge, such as where you found out that J.K. Rowling is the author of the *Harry Potter* books. However, if you excerpt or paraphrase an idea from a review of *Harry Potter and the Half-Blood Prince*, you should cite it. For instance, the following idea is borrowed from an *Entertainment Weekly* review and should be documented: "The parallels with current events are inescapable: Students are searched for dangerous devices before entering Hogwarts . . ."
- Cite non-text-based sources such as photographs, artwork, CDs, DVDs, TV or radio programs, ads, maps, and even interviews you conduct.
- Use your creative juices to present information in an "original" structure. For instance, this book uses the ABC structure to discuss evaluating sources. If you follow the exact same ABC structure for a similar document of your own, you would need to cite this book as the source.

REDUCE, REUSE, RECYCLE?

Ask your instructor for permission before you resubmit an essay or any other piece of work that you have already completed for another course. Even if you alter it a bit and slap on a new cover page, schools commonly forbid this practice. Recycling your research means doing less work than other students. You're also robbing yourself of the opportunity to learn something new.

Chapter 2

The Virtuoso Online

What do Britney Spears, Harry Potter, and MP3s have in common? They were three of the 10 most popular searches on Google in 2004.

While Britney Spears is rarely considered an academic topic, Google has become part of the tool kit for researchers, students and non-students alike. The Web is where people with questions go to get answers today.

There are billions of pages on the Web. Do a Google search for *horses* and you could get an eight-year-old's hobbies page, or a multi-million-dollar breeding business's advertisement, or a scientist's research about wild herds.

Quantity doesn't necessarily mean quality. Since the Internet is unregulated — anyone can post anything they want — you get the good, the bad, and the merely irrelevant. Can you sort them out? For instance, do you know the difference between paid and unpaid results? Can you distinguish between objectivity and bias, especially when the impulse reaction to a well-designed website is to believe its every word is the truth?

In this chapter you will learn the tools and tricks of effective online searching. You will also learn how to evaluate what you find, so that you get the most out of the Web.

SEARCH ENGINES: CRAWLING THE WEB

Search engines are a major tool for finding lots of web pages quickly. You'll find the websites for some search engines through the links on the home page of your ISP (Internet Service Provider); for more, see the list on page 22. Most are free.

The most well-known search engines are Google (www.google.com) and Yahoo! (www.yahoo.com). According to the Nielsen NetRatings, which provide Internet and digital media measurement and analysis, Google accounted for 46.2 percent of online searches (approximately 2 billion) performed by U.S. home and work web surfers in July 2005. Yahoo! was in second place with 22.5 percent.

Search engines index web pages by using a computer program called a **spider**. It "crawls" the Web and finds web pages by following one link to another. To learn more, log on to Search Engine Watch (www.searchenginewatch.com) to find listings, reviews, annotations, and search tips for search engines and other online search tools. Click on *Search Engine Listings* on the main menu bar.

To improve your searches, explore and experiment with different search engines. No one search engine will index every single web page out there, and every search engine works differently. But the basics of most search techniques are similar. Look at the search tips and help menus on search engine sites to find out how they work and how to improve your results.

Here are the search techniques you need to understand.

KEYWORD SEARCHING

Type terms or phrases — **keywords** — relating to your topic into the search bar. The search engine will find websites that include these words. Results are retrieved and displayed in a certain order. The ranking is calculated using a formula — which varies from one search engine to another — that weighs factors such as how often your search terms appear in an online document or whether they appear together as a phrase ("global warming" as opposed to "global" in one sentence and "warming" in another). Some search engines use popularity ranking, in which results are listed according to how many other sites link to each page; more popular sites are listed at the top.

When deciding which search terms to use, consider carefully what question you are trying to answer. From that, identify the key concepts and issues. Use the list you developed in your overview research and add to it as you learn more.

When you type in your keywords:
- **Use correct spelling.**
- **Use synonyms** (for example, if you are looking for *viewpoint*, try

also *perspective*, *opinion*, *stance*, *belief*) to get different results. A thesaurus might help you.

- **Use lower-case letters** to search for both lower- and upper-case terms.

CREATING RELATIONSHIPS IN KEYWORD SEARCHES

Use search "operators" to make your keyword search more precise. **Search operators** are words or symbols that create specific relationships between your search terms. Four techniques using search operators are listed below. Keep in mind that every search engine works differently, so not all these techniques will work all the time. Take a look at each search engine's search tips or help page to find out what you can and can't do.

PHRASE SEARCHING

Put words between quotation marks if you need to find an exact phrase or string of words. This is a good technique to use if you are searching for a name ("John F. Kennedy," "National Hockey League") or an exact title ("The Sun Also Rises"). You can also enter quotations of a few words or whole sentences to find their sources or commentary about them.

YOUREGONNAGETCAUGHT.COM

Turnitin.com is an anti-plagiarism service that is used by over 4,000 universities. An instructor can use it to compare a student's paper with *billions* of pages of student papers and other documents in its database. Turnitin.com then reports back on sections in the paper that may have been plagiarized.

It's even easier for instructors to do a Google test. If a paper has parts that seem just too brilliant or if the style is inconsistent, a teacher may smell trouble. Searching for phrases from the paper on Google could reveal the student's unacknowledged sources.

Taking the time to do your own work and to document your sources will almost certainly benefit you in the long run. A study published in the *Journal of Education for Business* found that "students who plagiarize less will be more likely to develop better writing skills, more creativity and greater self-confidence."

Use the Find function — hold down the CTRL key and press "F" — to locate a word or phrase within an electronic document. So, if you are looking at a lengthy document about Carl Jung, you can use this function to locate references to *animus* or *collective unconscious.*

BOOLEAN SEARCH

Boolean searching (named after George Boole, an English mathematician in the 1800s) uses the words *and, or,* and *not* between terms in the keyword search. Some search engines require you to capitalize these words (called **Boolean operators**); some don't. Verify this on the search tips page.

You can use Boolean searching to connect more than two terms, and you can use a combination of *and, or,* and *not* in the same search. You can even combine phrase searching with a Boolean search.

- **AND** — To find both terms. So, for documents about healing crystals, search *crystals AND healing.* The AND operator is the default for some search engines, such as Google. This means that any space between search terms is interpreted as an AND.
- **OR** — To find either term, or both. For the history of Microsoft, you might search *Microsoft OR "Bill Gates".*
- **NOT** — To find the first term but exclude sources that have the second term. If you are looking for information about natural disasters but do not want to read about tsunamis, try searching with *"natural disaster" NOT tsunami.*

WORD MATH

Place the plus (+) or minus (-) sign in front of each search term to create a relationship between terms similar to the ones established by using Boolean operators. As with Boolean operators, you can use more than two terms and both mathematical operators in the same search.

Do not put a space between the mathematical symbol and the search term immediately following it.

- **Addition** — To find both terms: *+human +cloning*
- **Subtraction** — To find the first term but not the second term: *+Walt –Disney*

• **Combined with phrase searching:** *"Star Wars" +"Empire Strikes Back" –"Return of the Jedi"*

WILDCARD SYMBOLS

Wildcard symbols can be helpful when you do not know the correct spelling of your search term. You can also use them to find results with multiple spellings or various endings.

A few search engines allow you to use wildcard symbols. However, this technique is more commonly used to search in databases (see Search Techniques, page 48). Every search tool has its own set of symbols and functions. Read the search tips page of your search engine to find out what you can and can't do.

The most common symbols are the question mark and the asterisk.

• **Use the question mark (?)** to stand for any one character. For example, searching for *wom?n* finds results containing *woman* and *women*.

• **Use the asterisk (*)** in place of a sequence of any number of letters. Depending on the search tool, you can place it at the beginning, middle, or end of the term, or do all three. For example, on OneLook Dictionary Search (www.onelook.com), searching for *politic** brings in results such as *politics*, *political*, and *politicians*; you can use **bird* to find *love-bird*, *songbird*, and *Thunderbird*; with *comp*tion*, you'll get results such as *competition* and *completion*.

ADVANCED SEARCHES

Use the advanced search option on a search engine's home page to make your search more precise. When you click on it, you will find options such as forms and drop-down menus.

For instance, Yahoo! has forms where you can type words into different fields to search for "all of these words," "the exact phrase," or "none of these words." These are the same functions as phrase searching, Boolean searching, or word math, but presented in a fill-in-the-blank format.

Other options in some search engines can make your search more specific. For instance, you can use a drop-down menu to select results that have been updated within various time frames:

any time, within the past three months, etc. You can also limit your search to websites written in one or more specific languages or to files in a specific format.

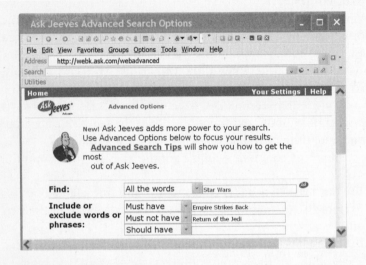

FORMAT-SPECIFIC SEARCHING

Use format-specific search options to find results in formats such as images, MP3/audio, video, and news articles. Most search engines offer these options. Look for tabs near the search box. For instance, if you click on the Images tab on the Yahoo! home page and type in *cats*, your results will be images of cats, with a link to the source of each image.

TRY THESE SEARCH ENGINES TOO:

- **Altavista** (www.altavista.com) — In addition to text searches, it has image, MP3/audio, video, and news searches. The home page also links to translations, yellow pages, and people-finder resources.

- **AOL Search** (search.aol.com) — Searches the Web or searches specifically for images, video, audio, or news.

- **Ask Jeeves** (www.ask.com) — Try its Smart Search features, which allow you to "search smarter" using links such as conversions, famous people search, product search, and stock search.
- **MSN Search** (search.msn.com) — Searches for websites, news, and images. Click on the Encarta link to search thousands of articles in the MSN Encarta online encyclopedia.

Search Engine Colossus (www.searchenginecolossus.com) lists more search engines from around the world.

Going back to Google, Dominic aims to be more efficient than he was the first time. He inputs *"genetically modified food" AND Africa AND famine* (phrase search and Boolean). The search retrieves about 31,000 results — way down from that overwhelming 4.5 million, but still a lot to consider.

One article from Worldpress.org reported in 2002 that several African countries had rejected U.S. food aid in the form of GM grain despite being in the grip of famine. The article picks up on several points Dominic saw in his overview research, so he prints it and saves it into his Favorites. He'll use the print date at the bottom of each page as the access date in his Works Cited list.

As Dominic does with all his sources, he evaluates this article using the ABCs of Evaluating Sources checklists (see pages 32, 53, and 69). From its About Us page he learns that Worldpress.org is "a nonpartisan magazine whose mission is to foster the international exchange of perspectives and information." He also finds a company address and verifies it on an online directory (www.yellowpages.com). "It exists, so it looks legit. What about the author?"

On the home page, Dominic types in the author's name — *Meron Tesfa Michael* — and finds 11 articles. The summaries show that they are about people and issues in the African region. So Dominic concludes that the author is knowledgeable.

As Dominic evaluates the content, he takes into consideration that the article was published four years ago. However, it is about a significant event in the timeline of his topic, so he views it as important material. The links on the home page are also functional and the headlines are current. "So the website is well maintained." With the Author, Body, and Currency all A-okay, Dominic decides that the source is reliable.

Dominic tries a search with a different term from his list: *agricultural biotechnology*. He finds an article titled "Science and Technology: Agricultural Biotechnology" on the Monsanto website (www.monsanto.com). It describes the benefits of biotechnology. The article is more positive about the science than much of what Dominic has read so far.

When he evaluates this source, he learns on Monsanto's About Us page that the company is a "leading provider of agricultural products and solutions ..." It is a well-established multinational firm that stands behind its scientific work. "They are in the business of selling biotechnology," Dominic realizes. The information may be useful anyway, but Dominic recognizes that it comes from a source with a particular bias.

On a different search engine, Ask Jeeves (www.ask.com), Dominic types in "*GM food*" +*Africa*. In addition to a list of results, Ask Jeeves provides a list called "Narrow your search." There he finds suggestions including *Solution to GM, GM Foods Stats, What GM Foods Were Sent to Africa*. Dominic clicks on the last one and a new and refined list of results is retrieved. He is impressed. "Here I thought that all search engines worked the same way."

METASEARCH ENGINES: MULTIPLYING YOUR SEARCH

Use a metasearch engine to search through several search engines and subject directories (see Subject Directories, page 26) at the same time. The top results from each search tool are then blended together.

For example, Mamma.com (www.mamma.com) allows you to simultaneously search through a variety of engines, such as Yahoo! and Google. The results are then displayed according to relevance, with duplicate pages eliminated.

The advantage to using a metasearch engine is that it allows you to get a broad scope of what's available on your topic with just one search. But the disadvantage is that it retrieves a large number of results, some of which might not be relevant to your needs.

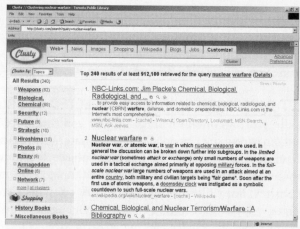

Permission granted by Vivisimo, Inc.

TRY THESE METASEARCH ENGINES TOO:

- **Clusty** (www.clusty.com) — Clusty organizes results into folders grouping similar items together, a process called **clustered searching**. For example, the resulting folders for a search on *nuclear warfare* will include Future, Hiroshima, and Photos.

- **Dogpile** (www.dogpile.com) — You can search for websites, images, audio, video, and news or click onto its Yellow Pages and White Pages tabs. Instead of pressing *Search*, you tell it to "Go Fetch!"

- **KartOO** (www.kartoo.com) — KartOO is a metasearch engine with visual display interfaces. After your search is sent to various search engines, the results are represented in a series of interactive maps.

- **Surfwax** (www.surfwax.com) — When viewing your results, you can click on the SiteSnaps link — it's a magnifying glass next to each result — to view a summary for any result. It includes information such as how many links, images, and words are contained in the selected web page.

- **Vivisimo** (www.vivisimo.com) — Vivisimo sends your search to major search engines such as MSN Search and Lycos and organizes the results into categories. For example, the resulting categories for a search on *Xbox* will include Reviews, Cheats, Codes, and Media.

SUBJECT DIRECTORIES: HUMAN-SELECTED SOURCES

Subject directories contain listings of websites that have been organized into groupings by people, not software. Whereas search engines use spiders to "crawl" the Internet, subject directories use information specialists such as librarians and editors to evaluate and index websites. So, while a subject directory contains a smaller collection of web pages for a topic than a search engine would find for that same topic, it excludes sites that experts have deemed irrelevant or inappropriate. In other words, a subject directory has done some of your work for you before you even click on it.

A subject directory presents you with a pyramid of subject headings. Broad subject headings — often arranged alphabetically — are at the top. They then expand downwards into narrower and narrower subheadings. Eventually you arrive at the bottom: websites about very specific subjects.

Take a look at Librarians' Internet Index (www.lii.org). This reputable directory currently has over 16,000 sources that have been evaluated at least twice. To see how it works, click on the broad category Law. It links to narrower subjects including Capital Punishment, Ethics, and Intellectual Property. Intellectual Property links to Copyright, File Sharing, Patents, and Trademarks. After clicking on *Copyright*, you will get a list of websites relating to that very specific subject. The librarians also provide a useful summary for each website.

TIP

The path of broad categories to narrower categories is called the BREADCRUMB TRAIL (Hansel and Gretel, anyone?). Law—Intellectual Property—Copyright is an example of a breadcrumb trail. Looking at these categories and subcategories may help you to define and focus your research by revealing how information specialists refer to your topic. Add these terms to your search list.

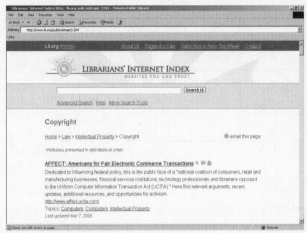

Permission granted by Librarians' Internet Index http://lii.org

Most subject directories also have built-in search engines that allow you to search their collections of websites. For these, you can use many of the same search techniques described earlier in this chapter. Click the search tips on the directory's home page to find out what you can and can't do.

NON-PROFIT VS. COMMERCIAL DIRECTORIES

Some search engine sites have their own directories. Yahoo! (dir.yahoo.com) and Google (dir.google.com) are two examples. Human editors maintain these collections of websites — which include general (i.e., non-academic) topics — and organize them into broad and narrow categories.

There's a difference between these commercially driven directories and the non-profit ones such as Librarians' Internet Index. Commercial directories are profit-oriented, so they include a wider selection of websites and may be trying to persuade you to buy things, such as books. Directories run by librarians and editors are intended for research and focus on more authoritative websites.

A 2001 survey by the Center for Academic Integrity at Duke University found that 41 percent of students admitted to cutting-and-pasting information from different Internet sources and piecing it together without proper citation. Over half of these students believed that what they did was not a serious issue. Every one of them was wrong.

TRY THESE SUBJECT DIRECTORIES TOO:

- **About** (www.about.com) — Find subject guides written by field experts in a wide range of categories, including Arts and Literature, Business, and Jobs and Careers. For example, the Pediatrics guide is written by a board-certified pediatrician and Fellow of the American Academy of Pediatrics.

- **Academic Info** (www.academicinfo.net) — This directory adds over 200 sources each month and currently has over 25,000 sources. Some of its featured categories include links to information about degree programs, test prep resources (for example, LSAT), and a student center.

- **Awesome Library** (www.awesomelibrary.org) — How awesome? Search and browse among over 25,000 sources in English and a dozen other languages. You can also choose different "entryways" into the site, designed for teens, parents, or college students.

- **BUBL Information Service** (bubl.ac.uk) — This directory indexes Internet resources related to all academic subjects.

- **Infomine** (infomine.ucr.edu) — This librarian-built directory is geared towards faculty, students, and research staff at the college level. You can search or browse among over 100,000 resources, such as databases, electronic journals, electronic books, and more.

- **Internet Public Library** (www.ipl.org) — Find links to websites about general subjects as well as ready reference tools, from almanacs and calendars to reading rooms and literary criticism.

- **Looksmart** (www.looksmart.com) — Find over 4 million websites organized into 300,000 categories and in 13 different languages. Click on the FindArticles link on the home page to search through millions of articles from academic, industry, and general interest publications.

- **Open Directory Project** (dmoz.org) — Search over 5 million sites organized into more than 550,000 categories. Over 65,000 editors, "net-citizens" who are experts in their subject area, volunteer their time to expand this directory.

- **Virtual Reference Library** (www.virtualreferencelibrary.ca) — This directory is maintained by the Toronto Public Library with help from library systems across Ontario. It has a special focus on Canadian content.
- **WWW Virtual Library** (vlib.org) — Tim Berners-Lee, the creator of the World Wide Web, began this directory in 1991 in Switzerland. You can find links to online resources relating to academic subjects such as Engineering, International Affairs, and Social and Behavioral Sciences.

On the subject directory Internet Public Library (www.ipl.org), Dominic clicks on the broad heading Science and Technology and then Agriculture and Aquaculture. One of the websites that comes up is Biotechnology in Food and Agriculture (www.fao.org/biotech), which is described as containing information "that may be of value to anyone interested in the role and impact of biotechnology in food and agriculture."

This website was created by the Food and Agriculture Organization of the United Nations (FAO). Its origins make it reliable, Dominic figures. One page he really likes is the FAO Glossary of Biotechnology for Food and Agriculture. That goes straight to his Favorites folder.

The site has other FAO documents. One of them is an annotated bibliography on the economic and socio-economic impacts of agricultural biotechnology in developing countries. Using Web addresses included in the bibliography, Dominic finds and downloads two reports.

Subject directories are really working for him, so he tries another: Toronto Public Library's Virtual Reference Library. He uses the search box to do a search for *genetically engineered foods*. He clicks onto the New Scientist: GM Foods Special Report page, which presents "in-depth reports on the subject of genetically modified foods."

Looking for more from this well-regarded journal, Dominic goes to the *New Scientist* website, which has a page about GM foods (www.newscientist.com/channel/life/gm-food). However, he needs a subscription to the site in order to read the complete text of its articles. He makes a note to search on his library's databases later to see if that article is available. Does he find it? See page 51.

THE DEEP WEB: HIDDEN RESOURCES

Have you heard of the deep Web? It is defined as the part of the World Wide Web that conventional search engines cannot access: the content found in online databases.

Research databases are collections of previously published information such as articles and reports. Many databases can be accessed only if you have a subscription; see Databases on page 46 to find out how your library can connect you to these. But deep Web resources can link you to thousands of others that are open to all users.

Online documents in the deep Web are more complex than the ones on the surface Web. Thus, conventional search engines miss them when their spiders crawl the Web. But newer technology is enabling search tools to run through databases as well as other websites. You can learn more about the deep Web in the book *The Invisible Web: Uncovering Information Sources Search Engines Can't See*, by Chris Sherman and Gary Price.

BrightPlanet Corporation, a private company that specializes in deep Web research, estimates that the deep Web is 500 times larger than the surface Web. BrightPlanet's Complete Planet directory (www.completeplanet.com) allows users to find 70,000+ databases with highly topical information in categories such as Agriculture, Engineering, and Social Sciences.

Conventional search engines are adapting to changing Web technology now too. For instance, Google has created Google Scholar (scholar.google.com), a search tool that lets you search on the deep Web for "scholarly literature, including peer-reviewed papers, books, preprints, abstracts and technical reports" from a variety of academic databases.

Another example is Yahoo! Search Subscriptions (search.yahoo .com/subscriptions). It lets you search "access-restricted content such as news and reference sites that are normally not accessible to search engines" (for example, *Consumer Reports* and *The New England Journal of Medicine*). However, you need a subscription to these sources to access the content, or you can pay a fee to access individual articles.

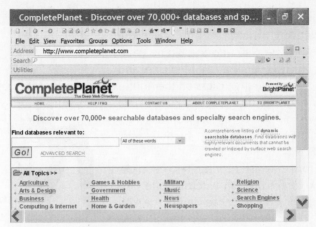

BrightPlanet Corporation www.brightplanet.com

TRY THESE DEEP WEB RESOURCES TOO:

- **Invisible-Web.net** (www.invisible-web.net) — The companion site to Sherman and Price's book, it mostly indexes free resources in categories like Business and Investing, Health and Medical, and U.S./World History, but it also includes some fee-based resources.

- **Profusion** (www.profusion.com) — This directory allows you to search from hundreds of specialized search engines and databases. For example, you can search for *human genome project* in the Biology subcategory of Science. Your search will be sent through resources such as *Discover* magazine and Bio Links.

- **Resource Discovery Network** (www.rdn.ac.uk/) — The U.K.'s free gateway is a collaboration of over 70 educational and research institutions, including the British Library. It links to more than 100,000 resources organized into 8 subject-based gateways. So, if you click on *Artifact* — the RDN's arts and creative industries gateway — you will find websites in categories such as Architecture, Fashion and Beauty, and Visual Arts.

Dominic goes to the Resource Discovery Network (www.rdn.ac.uk) to search the deep Web. He clicks on the Biome gateway, which covers Health, Medicine, and Life Sciences. He then clicks on the Agrifor link for Agriculture, Food, and Forestry. He narrows his search by subject headings: Food then Biotechnology then Genetic Modification.

From the list of websites, he clicks *Checkbiotech.org*, "an extensive site providing a broadly balanced view of the subject." Using the website's search box, Dominic types in *Africa*. He finds three articles, all published in 2005: "Genetically Modified Crops in Africa" (Reuters), "Biotech Corn in Africa Can Relieve Hunger" (*The Des Moines Register*), and "Survey Reveals South African Biotechnology Blind Spot" (SciDev.Net).

Dominic finds the first article useful because it summarizes several African countries' stance on GM commercial crops. The second one reports on evidence that biotech crops can help combat hunger in Africa. The third item is about a study that reveals the average South African citizen's lack of knowledge about biotechnology. He sees a potential connection between the average citizen's fear and the lack of knowledge about GM technology.

Dominic likes the article from SciDev.Net (Science and Development Network), so he goes to its website to see what else it has. On the home page, under Dossiers, he clicks on *GM Crops*. The jam-packed section provides current news, key documents (scientific studies, etc.), a glossary, links (to advocacy groups, international bodies, etc.), and more. "Wow, I really lucked out."

ABCs OF EVALUATING INTERNET SOURCES

You should evaluate Internet resources with the greatest care. The Internet is a vast source of information and so easy to use, but ...

Have you heard about the bonsai kitten? An authentic-looking website was once set up to sell bonsai kittens. The kittens were reportedly squeezed into a bottle. The poor creatures were fed chemicals through a tube to keep their bones soft and flexible so they would grow into the shape of the bottle.

Who would believe this joke (which in fact it was)? Well, a lot of people did. Soon, e-mail protest petitions were circulating. As this purr-fect punchline shows, not everything on the Web is legit.

Here are the key questions to ask when evaluating the **A**uthor, **B**ody, and **C**urrency of each source. It's particularly important to ask these questions when the source you are considering is not a well-known information provider such as an established media company.

Author
- **Who is the author?** The author could be a person or an organization. Unless it's explicitly stated on every page of the website, go to the home page by clicking on a link that says something like *Home* or *Home Page*. If there isn't a link, retype the URL (web address) up to the first forward slash (/). At the home page, you should get a better idea of who is behind the website.
- **What information is provided about the author?** The home page or the About Us page should tell you the author's credentials. What shows you that the person or organization has expertise, or is at least knowledgeable, about the topics on the site?
- **Is there e-mail, postal, or phone contact information that allows you to contact the author or a sponsoring organization?** By including contact information (e-mail at a minimum), the author provides some accountability for the content. These links also allow users to submit feedback or questions. You could use a phone directory to verify that the address and phone number match an existing person or organization.
- **What else has the author done or written?** What have others said about the author's work? Use a search engine site to search for the author's name (for example, *"Joe Smith"* or *"Society of Friends"*). You may find other publications by the author or websites that discuss the person's or organization's work. (Keep in mind, however, that there are other Joe Smiths out there!)
- **Is the website or its author respected and well known?** Use a search engine to do a link search by typing *link:* followed by the URL (web address), for example *link:http://www.joesmith.com*. The results will be websites that link to the site you're evaluating.

Click on these websites and take a look. Are the websites linking to your source credible too (such as an academic subject directory)? Why are they linking to this site? Is it because it is trusted, or perhaps because it has been discredited?

- **People posting comments on a blog, discussion forum (which is like an online bulletin board), or chat room can't always be checked out.** They may not even be using their real name. Treat these sources as interesting but not necessarily reliable.
- **Where is the site based?** The domain extension in the web address — the letters after the last period — might tell you. For example, *.com* sites are commercial, *.org* sites are usually non-profit organizations, *.edu* sites are academic, *.gov* sites are governmental, and *.ca* sites are Canadian.

Body

- **Is the information on the site accurate?** Can you verify the information in other print or electronic resources? Is it well researched? Does the site or page provide documentation for its content?
- **What is the purpose of the site?** For instance, a commercial site with lots of ads and banners is trying to sell you products. Go to the home page (retype the URL up to the first slash) to get a better idea of the goals of the overall site.
- **Did the site turn up in your search as a paid or unpaid result?** Commercial search engines generate revenue by featuring websites prominently for a fee. Paid or sponsored results usually appear at the top or right of the results page. For instance, a search on Google for *HIV* retrieved sponsored links that included a website selling home test kits. These sites may be completely legitimate, but they might not always be as relevant or appropriate for your topic as other sites that have not paid to be placed at the top of the list.
- **Is the information objective, or is there bias?** Individuals and groups use the Internet (and other media) to voice their views. So ask yourself: Is the information provided fair and balanced, or one-sided? For instance, what facts does the author include *or* exclude? Look at the source and how its interests may figure into the information. For instance, an organization such as People for the Ethical Treatment of Animals (PETA) gains members by per-

suading readers that wearing leather and fur is inhumane. With that said, biased information isn't necessarily wrong, but you should take the bias into account if you decide to use the information. Make sure you consider the other side of the issue too.

- **Even a "reliable" website may have areas of unreliable information.** For instance, the BBC News site's Have Your Say section allows readers to post their thoughts on current affairs; comments there are not backed by the authority of the BBC.

Currency
- **When was the information created, and when was it last updated?** Avoid using information from a web page that does not show a date of last update; you won't know how new or outdated the information might be.
- **Click on the website's links.** If there are a lot of broken links or images that don't show up, the website is not being maintained regularly.

PAPER PAGE TO WEB PAGE: PRINT SOURCES ONLINE

Many resources that were once available only in print — books, newspapers, journals — are now also online. The online search tools described in this chapter will help you find what you need. Access to some of these resources requires a subscription or user fee, but if your library has paid for access, you can probably use them without charge; see chapter 3. Libraries also have older printed materials that are not in online collections; see chapter 4.

Organizations such as educational institutions (Penn, McGill), government agencies (the White House, the House of Commons), and professional bodies (the American Psychological Association, the Royal College of Physicians and Surgeons) used to rely on printed brochures or the news media to tell their stories. Now most have websites where you can read or download their materials and communicate with them directly. These sites can be valuable sources of information.

ELECTRONIC BOOKS (E-BOOKS)

In 1999, Stephen King rocked the publishing world by becoming the first major author to release a complete work — his short story "Riding the Bullet" — exclusively in e-book format. In the first 24 hours he received over 400,000 orders. In 2005, 10 U.S. college bookstores began offering digital online versions of textbooks alongside print editions on the shelves. The pilot project offered approximately 200 popular titles from publishers such as McGraw-Hill Higher Education.

E-books are simply books available in a digital format. You can download them into your computer or onto an e-book reader. One advantage to using an e-book is that you can electronically search its contents easily and quickly.

EReader.com (www.ereader.com), an electronic bookstore and publisher, offers over 13,000 titles, including contemporary fiction and non-fiction. Most libraries have their own e-book collections or subscribe to e-book providers (such as netLibrary). Users can also borrow an e-book reader (such as Rocket eBook) and choose from a list of titles to download onto the reader. Most readers can carry 10 or more titles, while weighing the same as one book.

REFERENCE SOURCES

Use online reference sources to find summary information about a topic or to point you towards in-depth sources.

Encyclopedias (*Encyclopaedia Britannica*), dictionaries (*Merriam-Webster Dictionary*), almanacs (*Information Please*), and other traditional print reference sources are available online for free or through subscription. Your library may also subscribe to these resources so you can use them without charge.

TRY THESE ONLINE REFERENCE SOURCES TOO:

- **The Canadian Encyclopedia** (www.the canadianencyclopedia.com) — Find the complete text of the *Canadian Encyclopedia* in English and French, an extensive timeline of Canadian and world events, and more.

- **Encyclopedia.com** (www.encyclopedia.com) — Find over 55,000 frequently updated articles from the *Columbia Encyclopedia* (Sixth Edition).

- **Fact Monster** (www.factmonster.com) — Use this online almanac to find information on numerous subjects, including World & News, People, and Science.

- **MSN Encarta Dictionary** (encarta.msn.com/encnet/features/dictionary/DictionaryHome.aspx) — Type in search terms to find definitions. You can also use the thesaurus to find antonyms and synonyms of your terms.

- **University of Texas at Austin's Useful Reference Sites** (www.lib.utexas.edu/refsites/) — Find numerous links to websites such as almanacs, dictionaries, directories, encyclopedias, and more.

NEWSPAPERS AND MAGAZINES

Newspapers and magazines post breaking news and exclusive content on their websites. Most sites allow limited access, providing recent headlines (often from the past seven days) for free while charging a fee for older articles. Some websites are completely subscription based. But your library's databases (see Databases on page 46) may give you free access to current and older articles.

Most search engines and subject directories provide articles-only search features, as does Looksmart. Headlines from newswire services such as Associated Press and Reuters are available on sites such as Google and Yahoo! In general, these websites provide current coverage (Google keeps headlines from the past 30 days).

A great resource is NewsDirectory (www.newsd.com), which lists websites of English-language media around the world. Its listings include: 3,500+ newspapers (including the *Guardian* and the *Washington Post*); 4,500+ magazines in categories such as Business, Culture and Society, Current Issues, Religion, and Science; and hundreds of TV stations. MagPortal (www.magportal.com) lets you read articles from freely accessible magazines.

CHOOSE YOUR NEWS

News junkies can get home delivery straight to their screens by using RSS (Really Simple Syndication), which lets you subscribe to the online content that interests you. Instead of visiting media websites one by one every day, choose from the "feeds" offered by your favorite publications and networks, and the news will come to you.

First you need to get a news reader, or RSS reader, which is usually free. Some readers, such as Bloglines (www.bloglines.com), are Web-based, meaning you can use them anywhere with Internet access. Others, such as Firefox (www.getfirefox.com), are stand-alone desktop applications that you download to use on your PC. Then select your feeds from the websites or from search engines and directories that index feeds, including:

- **Feedster** (www.feedster.com)
- **NewsIsFree** (www.newsisfree.com)
- **Syndic8** (www.syndic8.com)

Keep yourself up-to-date with the latest academic websites. Sign up for free e-mail newsletters such as the INTERNET RESOURCES NEWSLETTER (www.hw.ac.uk/libWWW/irn/irn.html) and the one provided by THE SCOUT REPORT (scout.cs.wisc.edu/report/sr/current/). They will inform you about the latest academic and scholarly online resources. It never hurts to get a head start for your future projects.

ELECTRONIC JOURNALS (E-JOURNALS)

Journals contain peer-reviewed articles written by experts. E-journals are academic journals that are published and accessed electronically. The relative ease and economy of online publishing has encouraged many publishers to cross over into the electronic format. Some journals, like the *Journal of High Energy Physics*, are published only electronically. These are called **e-only journals**.

Some e-journals are available free of charge while others are available through subscription. Again, your library will likely subscribe to databases that allow you to see journal articles for free. Chapter 3 has more about databases.

FOR COST-FREE JOURNAL ACCESS, TRY:

- **Directory of Open Access Journals** (www.doaj.org) — Hosted by the Lund University Libraries, this directory indexes over 1,700 free, full-text, quality-controlled scientific and scholarly journals.

- **E-journals.org** (www.e-journals.org) — part of the WWW Virtual Library — is a directory that links to e-journal collections in over 30 categories, such as Biochemistry and Cell Biology, Economics, and Social Sciences.

• **JSTOR** (www.jstor.org) collects articles from over 450 scholarly journals in more than 40 disciplines. Free access is available at many academic institutions. Ask your librarian if you have access and, if so, how to use it.

TIP

Looking for an address or phone number? Use an online directory like InfoSpace (www.infospace.com) or Canada 411 (www.canada411.ca). A reverse look-up search will find a person or business when you type in the phone number.

FIND MULTIMEDIA ONLINE

Use the specialized search tabs or links on some search engines to find an electronic image, sound, or video file. See page 22 for format-specific searching on general search engines such as Google and Yahoo! Dogpile, a metasearch engine, also allows you to do audio- and video-only searches.

There are also specialized search engines and directories that allow you to search for format-specific results. Whichever method you use, keep track of when you accessed the files so you can insert this data into your Works Cited list.

TRY THESE ONLINE MULTIMEDIA SEARCH TOOLS TOO:

• **Ditto** (www.ditto.com) — A photo search engine.

• **Picsearch** (www.picsearch.com) — A search engine that lets you limit your search to find only images, animations, color, or black-and-white.

• **Singingfish** (www.singingfish.com) — The search engine that "only indexes multimedia formats," such as MP3, Real, Windows, and QuickTime formats.

TIP

When you download an image from the Web, be sure to look on its source site to find out whether it is copyright protected. Most images ARE protected, a fact that Internet users often forget or overlook. Any original creative work — such as a book, a picture, or a movie — can be protected by copyright laws. You must have the permission of the copyright owner before you can reproduce, display, or distribute the work, and you may have to pay a fee.

Chapter 3

The Virtual Library

Electronic versions of newspaper, magazine, or journal articles ...
news stories from the 1800s ... historical documents from centuries ago ... These are some of the online items you can find
through libraries.

The library down the street or on your campus uses the
Internet to offer you a huge virtual library. As the quality of online
information improves, academic libraries are increasing their
reliance on electronic resources. You can use these resources on
library computers or on a remote computer — at home or on any
computer with Internet access.

In this chapter we discuss the electronic resources found at
academic and public libraries, such as databases and digital collections. You'll see how resources in the virtual library are designed to
meet your needs as a researcher.

DOORS TO DATA: ACADEMIC LIBRARY WEBSITES

Open up a world of information by logging on to your college or
university library's website. Aside from providing information about
the library's services, these websites offer in-library or remote
access to the library's catalog and electronic resources. They also
often feature practical research guides for academic subjects. Try
the library websites of other schools too. Keep in mind, though,
that some resources may be restricted to use by the school's own
faculty or students.

ONLINE CATALOG

Use the catalog to search for what's in the library, including books, audiovisual collections, and periodicals. The catalog will tell you where or how to see what you need. Every catalog is set up differently, but they all have similar search systems.

Some catalogs also link you to databases. For instance, if you search for a journal that is in a database that the library subscribes to, the catalog will link you to that database.

See page 61 to learn more about how to use a catalog.

DATABASE ACCESS

Use the library's subscription databases to search for online articles and books. You can use databases in the library or from a remote computer. See Databases on page 46 for more information.

SUBJECT GUIDES

Librarians prepare subject guides with recommended resources and tips for researching particular topics. Most academic libraries offer these online or as printed handouts. They list tried-and-true materials evaluated by information specialists.

For example, on Yale University Library's home page, students can click on *Research Guides by Subject* to find an alphabetical list of subjects. The Women's Studies guide has resources that include: journal databases and indexes (such as Contemporary Women's Issues), reference sources (*Girlhood in America: An Encyclopedia*), and links to websites (American Association of University Women).

COURSE GUIDES

Some academic libraries provide guides for individual courses offered at their school. Librarians often prepare these guides at the request of or in collaboration with instructors. Like subject guides, course guides provide general research tips and list recommended resources.

For example, on the Pennsylvania State University Libraries website, students can click on *Research Tools* and then *Research Guides by Course*, arranged by course code. The research guide prepared for Energy & Environment includes tips on finding books, articles, transcripts, and technical reports, and lists some recommended resources with details on how to access those resources in the library or on the Web.

ONLINE REFERENCE

Look at the reference section on academic library websites to find general information about research. For example, Seneca College's Learning Commons Online provides information on plagiarism and citing sources. You can also find links to online reference works such as almanacs (*Farmers' Almanac*), grammar guides (*The Elements of Style*), and government resources (FirstGov.gov).

STUDENT RESOURCES

Many academic library websites have tutorials about general research-related topics. For example, Pennsylvania State University Libraries' website offers online tutorials on topics including Information Literacy and You, Locating Company Information, and Patents.

VIRTUAL HELP DESK

E-mail or chat with a librarian to get research-related help. Look for a link — its name will be something like Ask a Librarian — on the library's home page or other relevant pages. Students can chat in real time with a librarian or e-mail questions to get a quick response. Librarians can point you to potential sources, but they won't do all the work for you. *Too bad, huh?*

OTHER LIBRARY WEBSITES

Other types of libraries — for example, public and high school libraries — also offer their resources online, and some have many of the same resources as academic libraries, including databases and subject guides. Like academic websites, they might limit access to some of their resources to give priority to their own users.

Take a look at LibDex: the Library Index (www.libdex.com/country.html). It lists public, academic, national, and special libraries around the world. For more about different types of libraries, see page 60.

DATABASES: ARTICLES, BOOKS, AND REPORTS FAST AND EASY

Use your library's subscription databases to find electronic versions of recent articles and consumer or research reports that have been published in magazines, journals, and other publications. Databases contain current information — a newspaper article could be added to a database within days — but not much that was published before the 1980s.

For example, ProQuest Newsstand provides access to the full text of articles published in over 450 U.S. and international newspapers since 1985. There are also e-book databases — such as netLibrary or Books24x7 — that let you search for and read electronic books. Many general reference works, such as dictionaries and encyclopedias, can be found in databases too.

USING YOUR LIBRARY'S DATABASES

Most academic and public libraries subscribe to numerous electronic databases that their users can access for free from a library workstation or from a remote computer. Remote access to particular databases may be unavailable at some libraries because of the licensing arrangements with the database vendor.

Look at the library website's home page or menu bar for a link called Databases, Electronic Resources, or something similar. You need a username and password to log in and use the databases. At an academic library you must be a student registered in the school to obtain log-in information. At a public library you need a registered library card to obtain log-in information. Ask library staff if you need help.

Every database works differently, but they all allow you to search. Explore and experiment. Once you learn how to use one database, it becomes easier to learn how to use another. You will find that your knowledge of database searching and of the various databases will increase with practice.

A document in a database might look different from its print version. A magazine article, for instance, has columns of type and photographs in the printed edition; in a database the type will be plain and you may not see photos or illustrations.

Dominic heads for his library's databases to find journal articles. His library's "Databases A–Z" guide seems to have dozens of listings — he doesn't know where to begin. So he checks the library website's subject guide for Biotechnology and also asks the virtual help desk for suggestions. "OK, I'll use Expanded Academic ASAP."

CHOOSE THE APPROPRIATE DATABASE

To find information about your topic, you may have to search the available databases one by one. Most libraries' lists of databases are linked on the website's home page or menu bar. The listing may be alphabetical or divided by subject or category, and usually there's a brief description of what each database offers.

Look for the databases that best fit your needs. For instance, if you are writing an essay on same-sex marriage, it doesn't make sense to use Computer Database, which offers articles from computer and tech magazines.

Don't forget to look at the databases recommended by the subject or course guides on the academic library's website. Still not sure which databases to use? Ask a librarian for help.

TIP The list of results from your database search may have a check-off box next to each item. Click on the boxes beside the items that interest you to "mark" them. Then click on a link that says something like View Marked Documents. The page will reload and list only the items you have marked.

USE APPROPRIATE SEARCH TERMS

What is the question you are trying to answer? Identify the key concepts. Then check your list of search terms and see whether any other synonyms or related terms come to mind. Have another look in a dictionary or thesaurus.

For example, in the topic "The influence of the late Pope John Paul in popular culture," the key concepts are *influence*,

Pope John Paul, and *popular culture*. So your search terms might include the following: *Pope John Paul; influence, impact, importance, significance; pop culture, mass media, mainstream, tastes, trends, movement.*

Dominic's list of search terms has been growing: *genetically modified, genetically engineered, biotechnology, agriculture, Africa, hunger, crops, famine* ... He's been using wildcards where possible to pick up variations in phrasing, such as *modification* and *agricultural*. The most recent addition to his list is *transgenic*, which he's seen in some articles. A dictionary search confirms it is closely related to *genetically engineered*.

On Expanded Academic ASAP he starts with a subject search for *genetically modified foods*. Since he wants to find only the full text of journal articles, he selects two search limits: "refereed publications" and "articles with text (full-text)."

The database sends him to an alternative subject heading: Genetically Engineered Foods. He clicks on it. "Hmm, 50 articles." He has the option of viewing all 50 or narrowing down his results by picking subheadings. "I'll view the list."

SEARCH TECHNIQUES

Search databases using various basic and advanced techniques. Database search functions are similar to the search tools described in chapter 2, and some provide more sophisticated search options as well.

The basic searches are author, title, subject, and keyword. To find articles, you usually use a subject or keyword search. Any of the four types can be used for e-books, but author and title searches work well only if you know what book you're looking for. Remember, every database works differently.

- **Author Search** — Enter a name (*"Stephen Hawking"*, *"Amnesty International"*) to find works by that author.
- **Title Search** — Enter the title of a specific work (*"British pets in decline, iPods on the rise"*, *"New Scientist"*).

- **Subject Search** — Search by topic and retrieve results that are organized into headings and subheadings. These headings are defined by the database. Most databases provide a thesaurus or a subject/topic guide to help users define appropriate subject headings, subheadings, and related subjects. For example, a subject guide search for *virus* using Expanded Academic ASAP will retrieve categories such as Virus Diseases, Virus Genetics, Virus Research. For each option you can view a list of all articles, break them down into subdivisions (such as Analysis, Cases, Causes), or see a listing of related subjects (for example, rabies).
- **Keyword Search** — Enter terms or phrases that you want to find in the citation (bibliographic data), abstract, or text of an article or book. Most databases allow you to use a combination of search techniques, such as phrase searching, Boolean operators, and wildcard symbols (see Creating Relationships in Keyword Searches on page 19). Look at the FAQ, search tips, or help page to find out what you can and can't do.

Use an Advanced Search menu to limit the search and find more precise results. You can choose limits such as publication title, subject, or date range. For example, on ProQuest Science Journals you can limit your search to one or more of the publications included in that database. Check the complete list of journals and pick what you need.

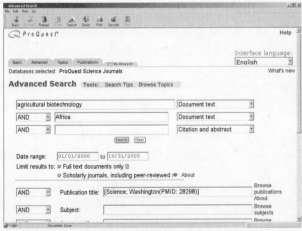

Image published with permission of ProQuest Information and Learning Company. Further reproduction is prohibited without permission.

Do you need to find articles written at the time an event occurred — for example, an election or a natural disaster — but don't know the date(s) when it happened? Use a reference source such as an encyclopedia to find out. You can then limit your database search by date.

IF AT FIRST YOU DON'T SUCCEED ...

Search results are listed in a logical order. For instance, articles are usually listed in reverse chronological order (newest ones first). You can usually choose to sort your results by relevance too. This means that results in which your search term appears most often are listed first.

If you're not finding enough results or have too many results, you have several options to broaden or narrow your search. Try a method like Boolean search or word math (see page 20). Key in less specific or more specific terms. Or use the database's search limits in the Advanced Search option.

In most cases you will find the complete text of an item or an abstract (summary) of it. If you find neither, don't fret. Use the bibliographic citation in the database — the item's author, title, and publication data — to see if the text is available in another database or in print at the library.

Still can't find what you need? Try searching in a different database. You can use deep Web search tools to search free databases (see page 30). For items published before the earliest date in a database, you can use printed indexes and the print or microfilm collections at the library (see pages 67 and 68). Digital collections are also well worth a look (see page 55).

TRY THESE DATABASES TOO

Not all libraries can offer these databases.

- **Academic Search Premier (EBSCO)** — Provides access to over 4,500 full-text journals in disciplines such as biology, chemistry, engineering, physics, psychology, religion, and theology.

- **Business & Company Resource Center (Gale)** — Provides access to millions of records that include company profiles, industry rankings, investment reports, and financial ratios.
- **Humanities International Complete (EBSCO)** — Provides the full text of hundreds of journals, books, and other sources from around the world.
- **LexisNexis Academic (LexisNexis)** — Provides access to full-text sources from over 5,600 news, business, legal, medical, and reference publications.
- **ProQuest Science Journals (ProQuest)** — Provides access to over 200 scientific journals covering a wide range of topics from the physical and life sciences.

Articles that turn out not to be in your library or online might be available to you through document delivery services. CISTI Source, for example, is a document delivery service with a focus on science and technology and health science journals. The items you want will arrive a few days after you place an order at the library. You might be charged a fee to use these services, and access might be restricted to certain users, such as faculty or graduate students.

As he finds each article, Dominic e-mails it to himself for backup and later reference. He also prints each one out. Although the bibliographic information is included at the top of the article, he records it anyway — author, title, periodical, database name, database service, library system, and access date — on his separate computer file as backup.

Dominic remembers that there was one article on the *New Scientist* website that he wanted to read but couldn't retrieve because he didn't have a subscription. But his library might have access through its database subscriptions. On the Expanded Academic ASAP search page, he enters *biotechnology*. Then, in the journal title limit, he enters *New Scientist*. He also uses the date limit, since he knows when the article was published. "Found it! The complete text, too!"

TAKING IT HOME

When the database gives you the option, e-mail yourself copies of the items that look useful. You'll be able to refer to them any time when you need to verify your information or cite your sources. E-mailing is usually free, and you'll save yourself the cost of printing documents in the library.

To print an article at home (or in the library if necessary), select the printer-friendly version. This option ensures that each article is completely printed and eliminates banners and other irrelevant information. E-book databases restrict the number of pages you may print from a copyright-protected book; usually the limit is a chapter.

The print date at the bottom of your printout is the access date for your Works Cited list.

TIP To cite a source found through a subscription database at a library, many documentation styles require the name of the database, the name of the subscription service, the name of the library or library system where you accessed the database, and the access date.

E-MAIL ALERTS

Some databases — such as ProQuest databases — let you set up e-mail alerts that will send you new information as it is made available.

After you have performed a search that gave you useful results (for example, *Pope AND influence*), click on a button that says something like Set Up Alert. Enter your e-mail address. Whenever new results are available for that specific search, you will be alerted via e-mail.

ABCs OF EVALUATING DATABASE SOURCES

For research purposes, you will probably use electronic databases a lot. One advantage of databases is that the articles, reports, and other documents in them have already been published elsewhere, so their original publishers have done some evaluation of their quality. That is especially true of journal articles, which are **refereed**, or **peer reviewed**; in other words, they are looked at by experts in the author's field before publication. In addition, the database services have filtered the items for reliability when they selected them to include in their products.

Since the documents you find in databases are electronic versions of print sources, evaluating them is similar to evaluating print sources. See page 69 for more detailed questions to ask.

Author

- **Who wrote the information?** What can you find out about the author's education, credentials, and reputation?
- **What else has the author written?** Try a search on the same database — using an author limit — which may locate other articles by the author. Book reviews may tell you what other people have said about this author's publications.
- **The citation will tell you the original publication source. Is the publisher familiar and reliable?** For example, university presses such as Oxford University Press are considered reliable.

Body

- **Is the information well researched and documented?** Journal articles, including the electronic versions, usually include notes and works cited. Popular magazines are less likely to show sources.

- **Is the information objective, or is there bias (see page 34)?** A biased viewpoint may be unavoidable, especially on contentious issues, but it can still be valuable if the source has some authority and the bias is declared.

- **As you decide which of your results will be most useful at this point in your research, look for some signals.** The abstract or summary will tell you how detailed the article is and how easily you will be able to understand its language and its approach to the topic.

Currency

- **If you need current information, check the document's date.**

One of the articles Dominic finds is "Landmark Report Aims to Lay Franken-food Scares to Rest" (*New Scientist*, 2003). It summarizes a U.K. government report prepared by a panel of both advocates and opponents of GM technology. All the panelists have impressive credentials. An accompanying sidebar lists what is known and not known about the controversial topic (health effects, for instance). "The report covers both sides of the debate, so it's balanced," Dominic says.

Looking again at the results list he got for *genetically modified foods*, Dominic realizes that some of the authors and journal titles are starting to look familiar. "That's good," he figures. "Authors who write about this subject often must have a lot of expertise.

"But I want to get lots of points of view ... How about this article?" He opens an item from a journal he hasn't seen before. The article misspells the name of the country it's about — twice in the first three paragraphs.

"Whoa! That one's not for me," Dominic decides. "Better stick to the ones that get things right."

DIGITAL COLLECTIONS:
SCANNING THE PAST AND PRESENT

Digital collections are special databases that contain items that have been scanned into an electronic (digitized) format. Using database search techniques, you can find books, articles, photos, and memorabilia and view them on the computer screen as they looked originally. Some digital collections also include audio and video recordings. Each collection is different; some focus on a particular subject, some aim to reproduce an existing print collection, some concentrate on rare artifacts.

Toronto Star Archives

Digital collections make it possible for users to look at facsimiles of historical documents that may be too fragile to handle. Digitization preserves for future users the content of knowledge from times past.

Most academic, public, and other libraries provide access to at least some of the wide range of available digital collections through database subscriptions. Some libraries have created their own digital collections.

One well-respected collection is called American Memory (http://memory.loc.gov/ammem/), at the Library of Congress. It has over 7.5 million items from the library's history collections, including Civil War maps, sheet music, early panoramic photographs, and government documents from as far back as the 1700s.

Major newspapers are also digitizing their archives. For example, the *New York Times* digital news database lets users search among over 15 million articles from as far back as 1851. So just imagine, you can find digitized articles written at the time of the *Titanic* disaster, the world wars, or the first landing on the moon. You can even see images, ads, and obituaries — not the sort of content that's included in an ordinary database — as they looked in the original newspapers.

PRIMARY AND SECONDARY SOURCES

Your instructors may require you to use a certain number of sources and may specify the kinds of sources (books, journals, etc.). Some assignments will include finding both primary and secondary sources. Do you know the differences?

Primary sources contain first-hand accounts and observations. Some examples:
• a novel such as Virginia Woolf's *Mrs. Dalloway*
• a diary such as Anne Frank's famous *The Diary of a Young Girl*, which contains the first-hand account of a girl's life during the Holocaust
• an original research report, which contains raw data obtained through experiments and first-hand observations
• a transcript of an interview, a speech, or court testimony

Secondary sources are works that offer analysis, evaluations, or interpretations of primary sources. Some examples:
• a literary criticism of *Mrs. Dalloway*
• a biography of Anne Frank, which may use excerpts and facts from her diary
• a journal article that analyzes an original research study
• a retrospective article about a famous person that uses quotations from previous interviews or speeches

PRESERVING THE JEWELS OF THE LIBRARIES

Libraries around the world have been digitizing books — albeit slowly and expensively — since the early 1990s. A recent example is the International Children's Digital Library (www.icdlbooks.org), a project of the University of Maryland. It offers free full-text access to over 800 old and new children's books that are available in more than 30 languages.

Are you an image junkie? Check out the New York Public Library's Digital Gallery (http://digitalgallery.nypl.org/nypldigital). It provides free access to over 300,000 images digitized from the library's collections. The gallery includes historical maps, vintage posters, rare prints, photos, and illustrated books.

Take a look at the links on Google Directory (http://directory .google.com/Top/Reference/Libraries/Digital/) to find libraries that provide digital content.

In 2004, a University of Georgia journalism student was caught plagiarizing after he wrote an article reporting on a recent bicycle race. Instead of providing his own coverage, he reported results he found on the website created by the organizers. Problem was, the results he lifted were from the 2002 race. *Oops*.

Chapter 4

The Information Warehouse

With so much information available on the Web and in virtual libraries, you may wonder whether there's any reason to get away from your screen and into a library building.

Actually, there are more reasons than you can count — and some that can't be measured. Libraries have the thousands of books, periodicals, and audiovisual materials you'd expect, including older materials not available electronically that you'll want to explore if you're researching historical subjects. In the print copies of magazines you'll see the colorful illustrations that aren't shown in the database versions.

Some libraries have special collections, too, that feature rare or historical items from the far past to the present. For instance, the collections of the Thomas Fisher Rare Book Library in the University of Toronto Libraries include letters, manuscripts, and an 1866 New York edition of *Alice's Adventures in Wonderland*, among other valuable items. Some of these rare materials are being digitized (see page 72), but they're not all online. And viewing something on a screen is not the same as seeing it in person. For the smell of history that emanates from the delicate browning pages of an early novel, or for the impact of fabulous photography in a glossy magazine — you have to be there.

In addition, libraries provide services such as learning centers and classes in research skills. Librarians and other staff members are there to help you with specific questions or just to point you in the right direction.

ACADEMIC AND PUBLIC LIBRARIES

In general, you will use an academic or public library for research. See the sidebar below to read about other types of libraries.

The library at your college or university may have more than one building. A larger academic institution will often have several branches holding its collections in different disciplines. Harvard University, for instance, has its medical school library, its Earth and Planetary Sciences Library, and its Fine Arts Library.

Public library branches are less likely to have subject-specific collections. They develop their collections and services to meet the needs of everyone in the branch's local community: students and other researchers, young readers, seniors, local businesses, and other library users.

A WORLD OF LIBRARIES

In addition to academic and public libraries, other libraries have resources to offer. LibDex: The Library Index (www.libdex.com/country.html) lists academic, public, national, and special libraries around the globe.

- **High school libraries** offer teachers and students basic collections of print and electronic resources. Collections are maintained and developed in close co-operation with teachers. School libraries are usually open during school hours and closed on weekends.

- **Government libraries** such as the Library of Congress are maintained out of central government funds and accessible to the public by law. A national library preserves the nation's culture and history. For instance, the National Library of Canada collects materials published in Canada and those about Canada published elsewhere. Other levels and agencies of government maintain libraries too.

- **Special libraries** are created and maintained by individuals, corporations, or other sponsoring groups. Access is often limited to people connected in some way to the sponsor, but researchers may be able to arrange to use the collections. Resources are usually focused on specific subject areas.

The information specialists at Bell Canada's Information Resource Centre provide services such as research assistance, user education training, and website maintenance for employees and subsidiaries of the Bell Canada Enterprises family of companies. Another, very different, example is the American Nudist Research Library in Florida, which seeks to preserve the history of the social nudist movement in North America. It includes books — like Dr. Seuss's *The Seven Lady Godivas*, which is about seven naked sisters — oral histories, and memorabilia. Clothing is optional.

TIP

Sign up for a library card if you don't have one already. It is your all-access pass to the library's resources. With a card, you can sign out books and access the library's electronic resources, either at the library or from a remote computer. Library cards can often be used as debit cards within the library, allowing you to make photocopies and printouts.

The computer workstations in libraries have several purposes. You can access the Internet on them (or you can use your own laptop in a library's wireless access zone). You can use basic software such as word processing; school libraries may offer course-specific software too. And you can use the library's online catalog, which is your guide to the whole information warehouse.

THE CATALOG: A MAP ONLINE

Use the library's online catalog to search for library materials. You can access it on library computers or from a remote computer.

Libraries that have branches or belong to a system of libraries usually allow you to search for items from all locations at once. For example, the Chicago Public Library's catalog lets you search in all of its 79 locations.

Dominic heads off to the Science and Technology Library on his campus, following the map on the library website.

On the online catalog, he starts with a subject search: *genetically*

modified foods. From the list of matching and related subject headings, he clicks *biotechnology*. One of the books he finds intriguing is *Food, Inc.: Mendel to Monsanto — The Promises and Perils of the Biotech Harvest* by Peter Pringle (2003). "It's pretty current, too."

Dominic tries another search using terms recommended by the virtual reference desk staff: *food supply—Africa—case studies*. One of the books listed is *Famine in Africa: Causes, Responses and Prevention* by Joachim von Braun et al. (1999). It looks useful. Unfortunately, it is signed out. "Drat! But maybe it's at the public library." The public library's online catalog shows it's available. "Good. I'll head there after I'm done here."

BASIC SEARCHES

Every catalog lets you search for library materials in different ways, and results are displayed differently on the screen. In general, you can use four basic search methods: author, title, subject, and keyword. Remember, *spelling counts.*

AUTHOR SEARCH

Enter a person's last name and first name (*Greene, Graham*) to retrieve a list of works by that author. If you know only the last name, enter it and the results will be all the authors who have that same last name (*Greene, Alan* and *Brenda* and *Charles* ... and *Graham*).

An organization can also be an author (*Modern Language Association of America*). Enter its name to find its publications (*The MLA Style Sheet*).

TITLE SEARCH

Enter the full title of the work if you know it — when searching for items from a reading list, for example.

Whether it is a book (*Jane Eyre*), journal (*Journal of Psychology*), video recording (*Citizen Kane*), or book series (*Chicken Soup*), the catalog will retrieve a list of all library materials with that title.

If you only know part of the title, enter that portion to find materials that have titles starting with those words.

SUBJECT SEARCH

Enter a subject to find a list of library materials related to that subject.

Catalogs use standard headings to describe subjects. You may find poems under Poetry, not Poems or Poets. But catalogs are designed to guess at what you mean. If you type *poems*, you will probably get a result that says, *See poetry*.

Most catalogs also provide you with additional subheadings and subjects related to what you've typed. Type *hunger* and the catalog might suggest that you *See also* other subheadings, such as Appetite, Fasting, and Starvation.

KEYWORD SEARCH

Not sure where your search term might find a match? A keyword search will cover a lot of ground. You will retrieve results that have your keyword somewhere in the title, author name, or subject heading. Some catalogs allow you to include Boolean operators (AND, OR, NOT) and wildcard symbols in a keyword search too (see pages 20 and 21).

For example, a keyword search for *Margaret Thatcher* may find results under an author heading (books by her), works with her name in the title, and materials where she is the subject, such as documentaries.

CALL NUMBER

Some catalogs allow you to do call number searches. If you know the call numbers (see page 65) associated with your topic — perhaps you have call numbers for books you've seen already — you can get a list of titles in the same location in the library.

ADVANCED SEARCH

Use the limits in the catalog's advanced search options to pinpoint more precise results. Some common limits are:

- Limit by **format** — journal, DVD, etc. — to find specific categories of items.

- Limit by **publication date** to find items published in specific periods.
- Limit by **language** to find items in specific languages.
- Limit by **location** to find items in a specific library or branch.

SEARCH RESULTS

Results are usually displayed alphabetically. When you click on a result, the full item record will appear.

This record provides information that will help you decide whether the item is what you need. It will also tell you where to find the item in the library (or if it's at another branch). Some of the important details in the record:

- **Format** — Is the item a book, a CD, a film?
- **Publisher** — Who published it?
- **Date** — When was it published or released?
- **Description** — How many pages is it, or what is its running time?
- **Notes** — What other description is provided about the source? For example, a record for a CD-ROM might include its registration number (which you need to install it on the computer).
- **Call Number/Location** — Where is it kept in the library or in the library system?
- **Availability** — Is it available today? It may be checked out or off the shelf for another reason, such as repair work. Can you view it electronically, in a database?

WHERE TO FIND IT

Use the call number and location information in the library catalog to find materials. In multi-level or multi-branch libraries, look for maps or directories you can use to find your way around. This information is usually posted on the library website, too.

TIP Find out about the different resources available in your library and how they are organized by signing up for a free tour. At academic libraries, tours are often arranged during the first few weeks of the semester. Academic and public library users can also arrange tours for themselves or for small groups. Knowing how the library works can help you become a more efficient researcher.

CALL NUMBERS

A call number is the address of a library item, in letters, numbers, or both. It describes the item's subject and tells you where to look for it. Each set of shelves in the library is labeled with the range of call numbers for the items stored there.

Call numbers are assigned by using classification systems that organize knowledge into broad categories, such as geology or literature, and from there into narrower subcategories. Academic libraries in North America mostly use the Library of Congress (LC) system; many public libraries use the Dewey Decimal system.

The same book can have different call numbers in different libraries. In a library using the LC system, *No Logo: Taking Aim at the Brand Bullies* by Naomi Klein might have the call number HD2755.5 .K57 2000. The same work would be labeled 338.88 KLE in a Dewey Decimal library. Even within one library, the call number may vary for different editions of the same work.

LOCATION

Together with the call number, the catalog's item record gives you location information such as the area or floor where the item is located. In a system with more than one building, you'll need to know which branch to go to. If there are several copies of the item, you can choose where to get one. Many libraries can bring an item you need from another location to the one most convenient for you, using a "reserve" or "intraloan" system.

OPEN SHELF

The designation "open shelf" means you can go to the shelf yourself to get the item. Look for the call number signs. Items are also organized logically: books are shelved with books, while separate sections are kept for other items, such as newspapers, periodicals, government files, etc.

Items are usually on an "open shelf" if they *don't* have any of the other designations below, even if the catalog doesn't specifically say so.

STACKS OR CLOSED STACKS

When an item is marked "stacks" or "closed stacks," it is located in an area where only staff can go. Write the relevant information about the item on a form and give it to a library worker, who will retrieve the item for you.

REFERENCE

Items in the reference section of the library can be used only in the library. These materials are heavily used (dictionaries, encyclopedias, bibliographies, etc.), so they may not be signed out. A reference item is labeled *R* or *REF* in the catalog.

COURSE RESERVES OR SHORT-TERM LOANS

The course reserves hold items set aside at the request of instructors. Like reference items, they are heavily used; students may be allowed to use them only in the library, or some items may be signed out for a short time. Course reserves usually consist of required and supplementary readings and lecture notes. In the academic library catalog, you can often search for course reserves by course code and by instructor.

REFERENCE WORKS

Reference sources can provide overview information or more in-depth information. Many reference sources are available online in databases (see page 46), but some specialized works can be found only in print, in libraries.

For more recommended references, see pages 8 and 36.

STATISTICAL COLLECTIONS

Use collections of statistics to find numerical data. For instance, government agencies are required to publish certain statistical reports. Most of this information is also available on their official websites. American FactFinder (factfinder.census.gov) provides population, housing, economic, and geographical data. Statistics Canada (www.statscan.ca) provides statistics about population, the economy, travel and tourism, and more.

TIP

Remember to look for print or online subject guides at the library (see page 44). They'll put you a step ahead.

BIBLIOGRAPHIES

Book-length bibliographies are compiled by scholars, librarians, or publishers to help researchers find published works about general subjects or specific fields of knowledge. For example, the annual *MLA International Bibliography* provides an organized list of over 66,000 books and articles published on modern languages, literatures, folklore, and linguistics. Some bibliographies have annotations that describe or evaluate the works listed.

PERIODICAL INDEXES

Periodical indexes list articles in newspapers, magazines, and journals by author, title, date, and source. For example, each volume of the *Canadian Periodical Index* lists articles published in Canadian magazines for a given period. You can also use its database counterpart to find a regularly updated list of articles in electronic format. Indexes for older periodicals may be available only in print volumes.

ABSTRACT COLLECTIONS

Use a collection of abstracts to find summaries of articles. For instance, *Historical Abstracts* covers internationally published journal articles about the field of history. Some collections include book abstracts too. The summary can help you decide whether it's worth looking for the full text in the library or in a database.

PERIODICAL COLLECTIONS

As described in chapter 3, articles in most periodicals going back to the 1980s are available in electronic databases. For older items and for periodicals that haven't been put online, check out your library's collection of microfilms or bound volumes.

MICROFILM

Before databases and digitization, newspapers and some magazines were converted and preserved on microfilm. Individual pages were photographed and reduced to fit on a strip of film. Reels of microfilm can be read on a microfilm reader, which projects the images onto a screen at about their original size.

BOUND VOLUMES

Print copies of many magazines and journals can be found on library shelves, bound together into hardcover volumes. For some popular publications, libraries continue to collect and bind print copies even though the text of articles is available online. These print editions allow you to see the colors and layout of the originals.

Some bound volumes are kept in the library's closed stacks, where staff can retrieve them for you.

POPULAR VS. SCHOLARLY PERIODICALS

A **periodical** has a fixed title and is published at regular intervals. The category includes newspapers (*Washington Post, Toronto Star*), magazines (*The Atlantic Monthly, People*), and journals (*Modern Pathology, Journal of Bacteriology*).

Your instructors may require you to consult journal articles as part of your research. At a quick glance, a journal and a magazine might look similar. They both have many articles, and they are about the same size. Library catalogs and database listings don't usually spell out which periodicals are magazines and which are journals, but you can tell by looking at these clues.

Journals (academic/scholarly periodicals)
- The cover is often formal-looking.
- The title is dry and formal, and may include the terms *journal, review,* or *bulletin* (*Review of Politics, Journal of Canadian Art History*).

- Acknowledged experts such as researchers, scientists, field professionals, and scholars write the articles.
- Each article is refereed, meaning it is evaluated and reviewed by peers or a committee.
- The content is focused on reporting and commenting on current research developments within the field.
- The content is aimed at an academic audience (researchers, scientists, etc.).
- The language is academic and includes jargon.
- Each article will usually include a bibliography and footnotes.

Magazines (popular periodicals)
- The cover is usually flashy, glossy, and colorful.
- The title is catchy and fun (*Rolling Stone, Vanity Fair, Wired*).
- Journalists, editors, and freelance writers mainly write the articles.
- The content is focused on current and popular topics.
- The content is aimed at a general audience and is often read for leisure.
- The language is casual and usually stripped of jargon.
- The inside is filled with photos, graphics, and ads.

ABCs OF EVALUATING PRINT SOURCES

Reference sources are generally reliable in themselves, and you can use them to evaluate other library materials — for instance, to spot-check the accuracy of an author's facts and figures. Here are more ways to evaluate the **A**uthor, **B**ody, and **C**urrency.

Author
- **Who wrote the information?** Look for author biographies in books, magazines, journals, and reports. A biographical reference work like *Who's Who in America* or a search on the Internet might also yield relevant information.
- **Is the person or organization well known and trusted?** What makes this author an expert? Refereed (peer-reviewed) journals review their

authors' credentials and expertise before accepting articles for publication, so being published in a journal is a sign of reliability. What can you find out about other authors' education, credentials, related experience, and other published works?

- **Who is the editor?** Authors who don't yet have strong credentials can build their reputation by having their work published in anthologies or journals that are edited by well-known authorities.
- **Who is the publisher?** Academic presses (Harvard University Press), government agencies (Statistics Canada), and many commercial publishers are considered reliable. Ask a librarian if you're not sure.

Body

- **Is the information accurate?** Verify it (for instance, statistical data, basics such as spelling, and statements that contradict other information you've checked) in other sources.
- **Is the source well researched and properly documented?** Not all types of publications have Works Cited lists, but are the author's sources acknowledged in some other credible way? Has the author used sources that look respectable themselves?
- **What have others said about the work?** Look at reviews in reference sources such as *Book Review Digest* or *Book Review Index* (which are available as electronic databases, too). You can search a database for reviews in such journals as *Booklist*, *Library Journal*, or *Publisher's Weekly*. You can also check out the editorial reviews on websites like Amazon.com. Both positive and negative reviews can be informative.
- **Is the information objective, or is there bias?** See page 34 for points you should consider.
- **Does the work include the type of information you need?** You may need factual writing or opinion pieces; primary or secondary sources (see page 56); comprehensive or summary information. Look at a book or report's introduction, or check a database or a printed abstracts collection, for an overview that will tell you about the work.
- **Is this work aimed at readers like you?** Look at the language (is it very academic or technical?) and layout (can you decipher the scientific diagrams?). Is the content too basic, too difficult, or just right?

Currency

- **When was the information published?** If you need the most recent information about a subject, database collections may have more articles to choose from than the print periodical collections in your library.
- **When was the source revised?** Textbooks, research guides, and reference works often go through several editions. A work that a publisher decides is worth revising and updating many times is clearly one that's well regarded. Just be sure you're using the most recent edition if you need current information.

Food, Inc. is located in the open shelf section on the second floor. Dominic flips to the back inside cover to read the author's bio. Peter Pringle has written other books as well as articles for reputable publications such as *The New Republic*. The publisher is also well known: Simon & Schuster.

"Is the content what I need?" he wonders. The introduction begins: "The book is for those who still have an open mind about genetically modified foods …" This tells Dominic the author's approach and assures him that the book is aiming for objectivity. From the book's index he can see that Pringle covers African aspects of the GM foods issue. "Another plus."

The author ends his introduction: "I've attempted to demystify the language, explain the science, and make sense of the scaremongering and the bland assurances …" That's the kind of language that a GM food novice like Dominic needs.

Checking Amazon.com on his laptop, he sees a couple of reviews. *School Library Journal* gave Pringle's book a positive review. So, with Author, Body, and Currency checked off, Dominic concludes that he's found a solid source.

If there's one really relevant book at that location on the shelf, maybe there will be others nearby, Dominic muses. Browsing the shelves has worked for him before. Two titles that catch his eye are *Pandora's Picnic Basket: The Potential and Hazards of Genetically Modified Foods* by Alan McHughen (2000) and *Genetically Modified*

Foods: Debating Biotechnology by Michael Ruse and David Castle (editors, 2002). Both seem balanced and are written at a level he can understand. "Three books already. Woohoo!"

TREASURES IN THE LIBRARY

Some libraries are fortunate enough to house special collections of rare or unusual items of all sorts. These collections are terrific places to find primary source materials (see Special Collections, below). For instance, the American Treasures of the Library of Congress house Thomas Jefferson's handwritten draft of the Declaration of Independence, Alexander Graham Bell's lab notebook, one of the earliest known baseball cards, and over 130 million other unique historical gems.

Digitization (see page 55) is making it possible for Internet users around the world to view many of these collections — although they may lose some of their magic on a computer screen. See below for more examples.

SPECIAL COLLECTIONS

Here are five library treasure troves from around the world.

Civil War and American History Research Collection
Chicago Public Library (www.chipublib.org)
Dating back to 1897, this collection contains over 1,600 artifacts from the Civil War, including munitions, original portraits, uniforms, rare manuscripts, and books. It's not often you find a cannon in a library — and this collection has two.

Collezione Romana
National Central Library of Rome (http://www.bncrm.librari.beniculturali.it)
Get a little taste of Italy. This world-famous collection features manuscripts, books, drawings, and photographs about Rome from the 16th century to the present.

Creativity and Innovation Resource Centre
Hong Kong Public Library (www.hkpl.gov.hk)
Do you like to think outside the box? The Centre has over 1,500 books and journals about creativity and innovation. It appeals to users seeking to enhance their creative abilities and to teach problem-solving skills to others.

L'Inathèque de France
French National Library (www.bnf.fr)
Let's get loud. This collection preserves French radio and TV broadcast productions. It now has over 65,000 hours of radio and television programming.

Osborne Collection of Early Children's Books
Toronto Public Library (www.torontopubliclibrary.ca)
Bedtime stories through the centuries. This collection includes a 14th-century manuscript of Aesop's fables, 15th-century traditional tales, 16th-century school texts, and Victorian classics.

WHAT'S SO SPECIAL?

In 2003, Edwin and Terry Murray donated their entire collection of 55,000 comic books, 500 role-playing games, and thousands of fanzines to the Duke University Rare Book, Manuscript and Special Collections Library (http://scriptorium.lib.duke.edu). The brothers had built the collection since their childhood. Their donation is now part of a library that houses over 200,000 printed volumes and 9 million items in manuscript and archival collections in areas such as modern advertising.

Special collections can also include photographs, artwork, maps, pamphlets, postcards, music sheets, audio or video recordings, and more. Libraries have built some collections themselves over the years. Researchers or artists can use the Circulating Picture Collection at the Toronto Public Library to find photos that cover all subjects and reflect changing trends. The library also has a collection of over 50,000 postcards from as far back as the early 1900s.

As Dominic loads up with his three finds, a voice announces over the PA: "The library invites you to the Sherlock Holmes Mystery Room on the fourth floor. Look at old editions of Sherlock Holmes novels and other mystery novels, manuscripts, and more." Dominic is a mystery fan, so he decides to make a detour before settling at a desk with his new sources.

When he enters the room, he notices the dim lighting

and cooler temperature. Bookshelves line three of the four walls, with a fireplace on the fourth. On the mantel are several Sherlock Holmes figurines. In a glass-fronted bookcase he spots *The Strand Magazine* for April 1911. "Fifteen cents! I wonder how much it would sell for on eBay today."

USING SPECIAL COLLECTIONS

Special collections may be cataloged separately from the main library holdings. Ask a librarian to show you how to use inventory lists or other finding aids.

For the valuable or fragile materials in special collections, libraries provide special treatment. You won't be able to sign them out, but photocopying may be possible. Delicate items might be stored in climate-controlled rooms to limit deterioration, and you'll have to wear gloves to handle them.

MORE LIBRARY SERVICES

Libraries offer additional services to help you complete your current projects or enhance your research skills.

INTERLIBRARY LOANS (INTERLOANS)

If your academic library does not have the item you need, check with your local public library. If you still don't have any luck, interlibrary loans might do the trick.

Use an interloan to order a resource from a library in a different system. You may be charged a fee, but the benefit might outweigh the cost.

In some library catalogs you can search for materials in other library systems. For example, Princeton University Library's Borrow Direct service allows students to search a combined catalog of seven academic libraries — including those at Princeton, Columbia, Cornell, and Yale — and order books that are not available at Princeton.

USER EDUCATION CLASSES

Sign up for user education classes to learn about basic or specific library resources. As online resources become abundant, librarians are helping users keep up by offering these classes for free. In the past few years, user education has become one of the fastest-growing services provided by libraries.

User education classes often take place in specially designed classrooms in the library. In academic libraries, professors or teaching assistants (TAs) often arrange class visits. In public libraries, these classes are usually offered on a first-come, first-served registration basis. Classes that have been offered at the New York Public Library include: Articles: Finding Them Electronically; Searching the U.S. Census Bureau Website; and Searching Financial Databases.

MEDIA CENTER

Want to film a skit for a group project? Need to show a video clip or include background music for an oral presentation? Some academic libraries have separate media centers. These typically have audio and video equipment that students can sign out, as well as collections of audio and video materials.

LEARNING CENTER

Need help with writing or editing a paper? You can book an appointment for one-on-one assistance with tutors recruited by the library or tutors from a campus service that works with the library.

The learning center usually has its own collection of references for researchers, as well as valuable handouts like subject guides or tips on writing a paper and preparing a Works Cited list.

Dominic predicts that he will finish his first draft in one week. He books an appointment with the learning center so he can get some guidance on pulling his paper together. Among other things, he wants to be sure he understands how to document his sources correctly.

He's been typing up notes on his laptop, being careful to use quotation marks when he's copying word for word. He doesn't want to get his own words and someone else's mixed up. Here's one passage he copied down from Peter Pringle's book:

From *Food, Inc.*: "The biotech industry proudly points to the rapid rise in acreage planted to transgenic crops. A few million acres were planted with GM (genetically modified) seeds in 1996; by 2002 the acreage had expanded to more than 120 million. But this is still a tiny portion — only 1.3 percent — of the total global cropland, and 99 percent of the total GM acreage was confined to only four countries."

Dominic knows he has to reword this excerpt in order to use the information correctly. He shows Cathy at the learning center his first try:

> The biotechnology industry boasts about the quick increase of land planted with transgenic crops. In 1996, a few million acres were planted with GM seeds. It had grown to over 120 million acres by 2002. Still, this was just 1.3 percent of the world's total cropland. Almost all of the GM cropland was found in four countries.

Cathy says, "Glad you asked. What you've done so far is just paraphrasing: it's too close to the original in the words you've chosen and the order in which you've put the ideas. More important, you haven't used proper documentation — you haven't said you got the information from Pringle. Let's clean this up before you're accused of plagiarism."

That's a load of trouble Dominic doesn't need. After all the effort he's put into his research, he plans to get the drafting right too. This is his rewrite:

> Between 1996 and 2002, the total global acreage of GM cropland increased from just a few million acres to over 120 million acres (Pringle 2). However, this only represented 1.3 percent of the world's total cropland, and almost all of it was found in four countries (Pringle 2).

"Nice work," Cathy says. "You're a fast learner."

ARCHIVES: GATEWAYS TO THE PAST

Archives are not usually found inside libraries, but they are closely related. Whereas libraries have mostly published materials in their regular collections, archives collect original, one-of-a-kind, and unpublished documents (primary sources), such as birth and death records, manuscripts, diaries, rare photographs, and maps. Archives and special library collections (see Treasures in the Library, page 72) have some of the same types of holdings.

Archival documents provide researchers with historical context and information they might not find elsewhere. For instance, a filmmaker might use archives to find photographs or artwork from the late 1800s to accurately recreate a scene for a film set in that period. An architect might consult old plans of an existing building for a restoration project. A lawyer might consult government records as part of research for a legal case.

If you have a research project that requires in-depth work in primary sources, ask a librarian for help in identifying archives that have what you need. Public archives, such as the Library and

Archives of Canada, are open to the public by law. In-house
archives, such as those held by individuals or private corporations,
usually have restricted access. There are directories and published
guides to various archives, and some online resources such as the
following:

• **The U.S. National Archives and Records Administration** (www.archives.gov)
  — Find information about the different National Archives locations across the U.S., which have federal government records.
• **Archives Canada** (www.archivescanada.ca) — Find descriptions of the
  holdings of hundreds of archival institutions across Canada. The
  site offers links to the archives' websites.

Some archives have online collections or other services that
can let you see copies of items in their holdings if you can't make
the trip yourself.

VISITING ARCHIVES

Be prepared: go to a library first to research your topic. You will
need key facts such as names, events, and dates to narrow your
search in the archives and make the best use of your time. Staff will
retrieve the items you request — there's no browsing, and you
can't sign materials out.

Instead of similar types of items (such as manuscripts or maps)
being placed together, as they are in libraries, archival collections
are grouped by who created the items (for example, a famous
writer or scientist). This arrangement principle is referred to as
provenance. Each group of items created or collected by a person,
group, government, or corporate institution is called a **fond**.

To locate the items you need, archives provide many kinds of
finding aids of varying complexity. One common finding aid is a
descriptive inventory (print or electronic). It gives information
about the individual or organization that created the materials and
descriptions of their chronological and physical scope and subject
content.

If you are interested in learning more about archives, take a look
at "Using Archives: A Practical Guide for Researchers," created by
Library and Archives Canada: www.collectionscanada.ca/04/0416_e.html.

Chapter 5
Grand Finale

After the research comes the writing. If you've been evaluating and documenting your sources all along, you should be able to concentrate now on analyzing what you've learned and turning it all into a persuasive piece of work.

Once you've completed a full first draft, give yourself at least a day before you start to edit. You need to look at the draft with fresh eyes. In *Making Sense: The Student's Guide to Research and Writing*, Margot Northey says: "Editing doesn't mean simply checking your work for errors in grammar or spelling. It means looking at the piece as a whole to see if the ideas are well-organized, well-documented and well-expressed."

Be honest with yourself about your work. Yes, it is hard to be critical of something you slaved over, but doing so will only help you improve it. If you can, show your draft to peers or relatives to get their feedback as well. They're usually better at telling you what you need to hear.

See the sidebar on page 81 for websites and books that can help. For the final touches to your masterpiece, follow this five-point checklist.

1. EVALUATE YOUR CONTENT

Make sure that you have met the requirements of the assignment. This is the first thing that Ron Stagg, professor and chair of the history department at Ryerson University in Toronto, looks for when he grades a student's work. "First of all, does it answer the question that's been assigned?" he says. "Is the answer clearly written and clearly organized?"

2. VERIFY THE FACTS

Go back to your sources and verify key facts and details, such as the spelling of names, the wording of quotations, statistics, dates, and so on. It is understandable that when you are rushed or trying to make sense of the information, you might get some part wrong at first. But don't lose marks because you didn't bother to review your research. "The classic case is, 'On July 14th, John Smith killed Martin Harris.' Whereas it's really 'Martin Harris killed John Smith,'" says Stagg. "That does happen."

3. CHECK SPELLING, GRAMMAR, AND PUNCTUATION

Double-check your spelling, grammar, and punctuation. Make time to read through your assignment to catch the mistakes that spell-check doesn't (*your* vs. *you're*, for instance). Also, pay attention to flow. Have you written transitional sentences to help connect the ideas in the paper?

4. POLISH YOUR DOCUMENTATION

Make sure that you have properly cited all the information that you gathered from other sources, both within your text and in your Works Cited list. Have you used the style your instructor specified? Did you use that style correctly? Have you done more than just paraphrasing where you have relied on the work of other writers? "Make sure the words used are yours except where you are quoting," adds Stagg.

5. THINK ABOUT PRESENTATION

Make your project presentable. Prepare a cover page that clearly states the title of the assignment, your instructor's name, your name, the name of the course, the date, and other relevant information (according to the required style guide). Have you double-spaced your text and numbered all the pages? Is your last name (or full name) on every page? Have you inserted all the pictures, graphs, and diagrams you planned to include? Check the required format to make sure you've followed all the rules and included all the necessary items, page by page.

RECOMMENDED RESOURCES ON RESEARCH AND WRITING

This book lists many resources for researchers and writers, including your academic library's website, learning center, and staff members. Here are a few more:

- *How to Write a Term Paper* (www.gale.com/free_resources/term_paper) — Information about choosing a topic, crafting a thesis, taking efficient notes, drafting and revising a paper, documenting sources, and more.
- *The Writing Center* (www.wisc.edu/writing/Handbook/) — Information and resources about the stages of the writing process, grammar and punctuation, documentation styles, and more.
- Berry, Ralph. *The Research Project — How to Write It*. 5th ed. New York: Routledge, 2004.
- Booth, Wayne, et al. *The Craft of Research*. 2nd ed. Chicago: University of Chicago Press, 2003.
- Gibaldi, Joseph. *MLA Handbook for Writers of Research Papers*. 6th ed. New York: Modern Language Association of America, 2003.
- Northey, Margot, and Joan McKibbin. *Making Sense: A Student's Guide to Research and Writing*. 5th ed. New York: Oxford University Press, 2005.
- Soles, Derek. *The Essentials of Academic Writing*. New York: Houghton Mifflin, 2005.
- Strunk, William, Jr., and E.B. White. *The Elements of Style*. 4th ed. Boston: Allyn and Bacon, 2003.

Dominic checks and double-checks, takes all his sister's comments seriously, and hands in a nice neat paper — on time (unlike some of his classmates).

At the end of class three weeks later, he gets his paper back. He feverishly flips to the last page. He closes one eye as the open one scans the page for the mark. "A-minus!" His heart jumps.

"Solid analysis," the instructor has written. "I appreciate the recent data you've provided, which answers many of the issues ..."

Dominic grins as he files the paper into his backpack. "Couldn't have said it better myself!"

Works Cited

Unless otherwise stated, the information in this book was drawn from the Toronto Public Library's resources.

CHAPTER 1

"Art." *Quoteland.com.* 2001. Quoteland.com, Inc. 30 Sept. 2005 <http://www.quoteland.com>.

Farnum, Cecile. Phone Interview. 20 Sept. 2005.

"Misuse of Sources." *Faculty of Arts and Sciences, Harvard.* President and Fellows of Harvard College. 13 June 2005 <http://www.fas.harvard.edu/~expos/sources/chap3.html>.

Paolini, Christopher. "Prince of Darkness: J.K. Rowling's *Harry Potter and the Half-Blood Prince* casts its spell on guest critic Christopher Paolini." *Entertainment Weekly* 29 July 2005: 72.

CHAPTER 2

"2004 Year-End Google Zeitgeist." *Google.* 22 Dec. 2004. Google. 4 April 2005 <http://www.google.com/press/zeitgeist2004.html>.

"About Google Scholar." *Google.* Google. 18 Aug. 2005 <http://scholar.google.com/scholar/about.html>.

Brooks, Clifford. "Stephen King: King of the Ebooks." *Computing Unplugged Magazine.* ZATZ Publishing. 17 May 2005 <http://www.pocketpclife.com/issuesprint/issue200004/ebook.html>.

"The Deep Web." *University at Albany.* 6 Dec. 2004. University at Albany. 30 Sept. 2005 <http://library.albany.edu/internet/deepweb.html>.

"Deep Web FAQ." *BrightPlanet.* BrightPlanet Corporation. 30 Sept. 2005 <http://www.brightplanet.com/deepcontent/deep_web_faq.asp>.

"E-textbooks Hit Shelves." *Metro* 17 Aug. 2005: 18.

Finkel, Ed. "Sticky Fingers on the Information Superhighway." *Community College Week* 28 Feb. 2005: 6+. *General Reference Center Gold.* Gale. Toronto Public Library. 13 June 2005 <http://www.galegroup.com>.

Foxworthy, Natalie. "U. Cincinnati: Online Plagiarism on Rise, Officials Catching On." *The America's Intelligence Wire* 13 Jan. 2005. *General Reference Center Gold.* Gale. Toronto Public Library. 13 June 2005 <http://www.galegroup.com>.

Huber, Charles F. "Electronic Journal Publishers: A Reference
Librarian's Guide." *UCSB Libraries*. 2000. University of
California Santa Barbara Libraries. 17 May 2005 <http://www
.library.ucsb.edu/istl/00-summer/article2.html>.

Keith, Kimberly L. "Beyond Google ... the Deep Web for Parents."
About. About, Inc. 18 Aug. 2005 <http://childparenting
.about.com/od/familycomputer/a/deepwebparents_p.htm>.

"Nielsen NetRatings Search Engines Ratings." *Search Engine
Watch*. Ed. Danny Sullivan. 23 Aug. 2005. Jupitermedia
Corporation. 21 Sept. 2005 <http://www.searchenginewatch
.com/reports/print.php/34701_2156451>.

O'Daniel, Maria. "Lessons From 'Bonsai Kitten' hoax." *Asia Africa
Intelligence Wire* 10 Nov. 2003. *General Reference Center
Gold*. Gale. Toronto Public Library. 16 June 2005
<http://www.galegroup.com>.

"RSS Feeds." *Globeandmail.com*. 2005. Bell Globemedia Publishing
Inc. 16 May 2005 <http://www.theglobeandmail.com/rss>.

Sherman, Chris and Gary Price. "The Invisible Web." *Searcher*
June 2001: 62+. *Computer Database*. Gale. Toronto Public
Library. 30 Sept. 2005 <http://www.galegroup.com>.

Wiley, Phil. "Why Stephen King has Just Boosted Your Income."
IBoost. iBoost Technology, Inc. 17 May 2005 <http://www
.iboost.com/profit/other_revenue_streams/ebooks/03113.htm>.

"Yahoo! Search." *Yahoo!* Yahoo! Inc. 18 Aug. 2005
<http://search.yahoo.com/subscriptions>.

CHAPTER 3
"Article Archive: 1851–1980." *The New York Times*. 2005. The
New York Times Company. 30 Sept. 2005 <http://pqasb
.pqarchiver.com/nytimes/advancedsearch.html>.

"British Pets in Decline, iPods on the Rise." *UPI NewsTrack*
16 June 2005. *General Reference Center Gold*. Gale. Toronto
Public Library. 30 Sept. 2005 <http://www.galegroup.com>.

"Interlibrary Loan and Document Delivery." *Ryerson University
Library*. 20 May 2005. Ryerson University Library. 30 Sept.
2005 <http://www.ryerson.ca/library/info/illdd/>.

Ishizuka, Kathy. "Showing Google the Way: Digitizing Books
is Nothing New. Just Ask the International Children's Digital
Library." *School Library Journal* 51.2 (2005): 26+. *General
Reference Center Gold*. Gale. Toronto Public Library. 24 May
2005 <http://www.galegroup.com>.

"Plagiarizing Students Unable to Graduate." *The Quill* 92.5 (2004): 63. *General Reference Center Gold*. Gale. Toronto Public Library. 17 Dec. 2005 <http://www.galegroup.com>.

"Primary vs. Secondary." *University of Georgia Libraries*. 12 Dec. 2003. University of Georgia. 26 May 2005 <http://www.libs.uga.edu/researchcentral/choosing/what/primary.html>.

"ProQuest Newsstand." *ProQuest Information and Learning*. ProQuest Information and Learning Company. 30 Sept. 2005 <http://www.proquest.com/products/pd-product-newsstand.shtml>.

"What is a Primary Source?" *Princeton University*. The Trustees of Princeton University. 26 May 2005 <http://www.princeton.edu/~refdesk/primary2.html>.

CHAPTER 4

"About the National Archives." *The US National Archives & Records Administration*. 2005. USA. 12 Aug. 2005 <http://www.archives.gov/about>.

"American Nudist Research Library: More than Memorabilia." *American Nudist Research Library*. 2005. American Nudist Research Library. 30 Sept. 2005 <http://www.aanr.com/anrl/>.

Balas, Janet I. "And What of Special Collections in the Digital Library?" *Computers in Libraries* April 2002: 40+. *General Reference Center Gold*. Gale. Toronto Public Library. 3 Aug. 2005 <http://www.galegroup.com>.

Boyd, Stephanie. Phone Interview. 9 Aug. 2005.

Boyd, Stephanie. "What's Next? For Corporate Virtual Libraries: The Elimination of a Paper Collection and the Need for a Walk-In Library Space Frees the Information Specialist to Choose Their Optimal Work Space." *Online* Nov.–Dec. 2004: 14+. *General Reference Center Gold*. Gale. Toronto Public Library. 3 Aug. 2005 <http://www.galegroup.com>.

"The Collections." *Rare Book, Manuscript, and Special Collections Library Duke University*. 14 Jan. 2002. Duke University Libraries. 9 Aug. 2005 <http://scriptorium.lib.duke.edu/collections.html>.

"Comics to Duke." *American Libraries* August 2003: 25. *General Reference Center Gold*. Gale. Toronto Public Library. 3 Aug. 2005 <http://www.galegroup.com>.

Donaldson, Kelly. Personal Interview. 26 May 2005.

"Exhibition Sections." *American Treasures of the Library of Congress.* 5 July 2005. Library of Congress. 30 Sept. 2005 <http://www.loc.gov/exhibits/treasures>.

Farnum, Cecile. Personal Interview. 31 May 2005.

Frastacky, Luba. Personal Interview. 8 Aug. 2005.

Gibaldi, Joseph. *MLA Handbook for Writers of Research Papers.* 6th ed. New York: The Modern Language Association of America, 2003. 25.

"MLA International Bibliography." *MLA.* 17 Nov. 2004. Modern Language Association. 31 May 2005 <http://www.mla.org/bibliography>.

Prytherch, Ray. *Harrod's Librarians' Glossary and Reference Book.* 9th ed. Vermont: Gower, 2000.

Shantz, Mary. Personal Interview. 8 Aug. 2005.

Sherlock, Lisa. Personal Interview. 27 May 2005.

Singer, Lisa. Personal Interview. 9 Aug. 2005.

"Using Archives: A Practical Guide for Researchers." *Library and Archives Canada.* 2 Sept. 2003. Canada. 9 Aug. 2005 <http://www.collectionscanada.ca/04/0416_e.html>.

CHAPTER 5
Gibaldi, Joseph. *MLA Handbook for Writers of Research Papers.* 6th ed. New York: The Modern Language Association of America, 2003. 48–59.

Northey, Margot and Joan McKibbin. *Making Sense: A Student's Guide to Research and Writing.* 5th ed. New York: Oxford University Press, 2005.

Stagg, Ron. Telephone Interview. 15 June 2005.

ABCs OF EVALUATING SOURCES (CHAPTERS 2–4)
Cramer, Steve. "Evaluating Web Pages." *Duke University Libraries.* 14 July 2003. Duke University Libraries. 30 Sept. 2005 <http://www.lib.duke.edu/libguide/evaluating_web.htm>.

"Critical Evaluation of Resources." *University of California Berkeley Library.* 7 Jan. 2005. Regents of the University of California. 1 June 2005 <http://www.lib.berkeley.edu/TeachingLib/Guides/Evaluation.html>.

"Evaluating Sources of Information." *Purdue University's Online Writing Lab*. OWL at Purdue University and Purdue University. 1 June 2005 <http://owl.english.purdue.edu/handouts/research/ r_evalsource.html>.

"Evaluation Criteria." *NMSU Library*. 24 May 2005. New Mexico State University Library. 1 Jan. 2005 <http://lib.nmsu.edu/ instruction/evalcrit.html>.

Ormondroyd, Joan. "Critically Analyzing Information Sources." *Cornell University Library*. Ed. Michael Engle and Tony Cosgrave. 6 Oct. 2004. Cornell University Library. 1 June 2005 <http://www.library.cornell.edu/olinuris/ref/research/skill26.htm>.

DOMINIC: THE BUDDING VIRTUOSO

"About Us: Opening the Door to New Possibilities." *Monsanto*. 2005. Monsanto Company. 19 Aug. 2005 <http://www .monsanto.com>.

"About Worldpress.org." *Worldpress.org*. Worldpress.org. 29 Sept. 2005 <http://www.worldpress.org/about.cfm>.

"Biotechnology." *Encyclopedia.com*. 2005. HighBeam Research, Inc. 15 Sept. 2005 <http://www.encyclopedia.com/html/ b1/biotech.asp>.

Brasher, Phillip. "Biotech Corn in Africa Can Relieve Hunger." *Checkbiotech.org*. 15 May 2005. Checkbiotech.org. 7 July 2005 <http://www.checkbiotech.org/blocks/dsp_docToPrint .cfm?doc_id=10330>.

Coghlan, Andy and Nicola Jones. "Landmark Report Aims to Lay Frankenfood Scares to Rest." *New Scientist* 26 July 2003: 6+. *Expanded Academic ASAP*. Gale. Toronto Public Library. 8 July 2005 <http://www.galegroup.com>.

"Economic Statistics by Country, 2004." *Infoplease*. 2005. Pearson Education, Inc. 19 Sept. 2005 <http://www.infoplease.com/ ipa/A0874911.html>.

"Food, Inc.: Mendel to Monsanto — The Promises and Perils of the Biotech Harvest." *Amazon.com*. 2005. Amazon.com. 11 July 2005 <http://www.amazon.com>.

"Genetic Engineering." *Encyclopedia.com*. 2005. HighBeam Research, Inc. 15 Sept. 2005 <http://www.encyclopedia .com/html/g1/genet-en.asp>.

"Genetic Modification." *Agrifor*. 2005. University of Nottingham. 29 Sept. 2005 <http://agrifor.co.uk>.